INTERIOR
DESIGN
COURSE

INTERIOR DESIGN
COURSE

Tomris Tangaz

A QUARTO BOOK

Copyright © 2006 by Quarto Inc.

First edition for North America published in 2006 by Barron's Educational Series, Inc.

All inquiries should be addressed to:
Barron's Educational Series, Inc.
250 Wireless Boulevard
Hauppauge, New York 11788
www.barronseduc.com

ISBN-13: 978-0-7641-3259-9
ISBN: 0-7641-3259-8

Library of Congress Control no. 2005920489

QUAR.ICO

Conceived, designed, and produced by
Quarto Publishing plc
The Old Brewery
6 Blundell Street
London
N7 9BH

Senior editor: Susie May
Art editor: Sheila Volpe
Assistant art director: Penny Cobb
Designer: Andrew Easton
Photography: Martin Norris
Copy editor: Diana Lodge
Proofreader: Tracie Davis
Indexer: Pamela Ellis

Art director: Moira Clinch
Publisher: Paul Carslake

Manufactured by Provision Pte Ltd, Singapore
Printed in China by Toppan Leefung Printing Ltd

9 8 7 6 5 4

contents

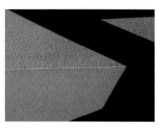

Chapter **1**

CONCEPT DEVELOPMENT **10**

Chapter **2**

DESIGN REALIZATION **32**

Chapter 3

DESIGN PROJECTS 68

Chapter 4

BUILDING CONSTRUCTION 82

Chapter 5

PROFESSIONAL PRACTICE 122

Introduction

Interior design is a social activity—it brings people together, allows us to communicate our ideas more effectively and to share our interests in a creative way. An interior designer has the rewarding task of making a meaningful impact upon the quality of individual lives by making qualities real. If you are reading this book, the chances are that you are already aspiring to make a difference.

Whether you are keen to develop your interest in interior design and build your skills, or to pursue a career and begin a portfolio, then this book is for you. Specifically designed to cover all aspects of interior design, this intensive course introduces the practice of basic design principles through set projects. Inspiration and imagination are the first key steps to starting your study. Whatever your background, this course will encourage your individual creativity and help you to explore and further your own design ideas.

The Interior Design Course introduces you to a specialized field where you will learn real skills from design professionals. Set out in units, this book follows the structure of a college course, allowing an in-depth and methodical approach to the discipline. Professional advice throughout this book takes various forms. Student portfolios guide your learning, while contemporary professional case studies give an insight into the nature and breadth of each specialist field to ensure the advancement of your practice.

Each chapter offers a series of projects to get you started and to help you to develop your creative, technical, and professional skills. Through a range of media, materials, tools, and technical and creative processes, you will gain an awareness of the design process and the importance of design issues.

The process of writing this book has been the culmination of many valuable experiences, first as an interior design student, a practicing professional, and then as a design lecturer, writer, and course director. I am grateful for these experiences and for the rich contribution made by colleagues, peers, and my students over the years who have questioned, tested, and stretched the intensity and complexity of interior design as a creative discipline. I hope that your experience of this book will be just as valuable and that it will inspire you to approach the subject with as much enthusiasm and passion—remember, design is not just about problem solving! It is about learning to understand and enjoy our immediate environments by helping to improve and shape them.

Tomris Tangaz

How to use this book

Organized into tutorial units to reflect the courses of top design colleges, this book presents all aspects of interior design, from the initial idea to adding the finishing touches. The content begins with a section on how to develop an idea, before explaining how to build on an initial concept (developing freehand drawing skills), and the practicalities of realizing a design (drawing up a survey and building client profiles). The last section shows you how to put together a portfolio and pitch at companies to get your first toehold in the business.

TUTORIAL UNITS

Content is organized into self-contained and easy-to-digest numbered units, which run for two or four pages. All the information connected with that unit is at your fingertips. These tutorial units deal with theoretical and practical topics.

PROJECTS

Each chapter offers a series of projects that allow you to practice your skills as you go along, and help you to develop your creative, technical, and professional abilities.

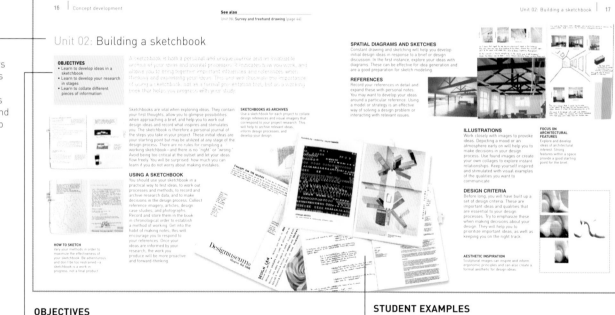

OBJECTIVES

Each unit's objectives are explained at the beginning. These give an idea of the topics you'll learn about in the following pages.

STUDENT EXAMPLES

The pages are packed with student examples, so you can compare your own work with that of your peers.

SPECIALLY COMMISSIONED STEP-BY-STEP SEQUENCES
Specially photographed sequences provide you with practical tools for making models, and give insights into technical drawing.

CASE STUDIES
The author looks at how interior designers in professional practice have tackled specific tasks, giving an idea of the brief and the budget. These case studies will inspire your own designs and provide a valuable insight into the work of the professional designer.

SPIRAL STAIRCASES
A spiral staircase with a central newel can be made very easily using the following method. Draw the stair plan on card. Cut the circles, but leave the newel hole. Make a jig of card to hold the newel horizontal. Mark up the newel with risers. Cut a bird mouth to allow for the newel hole. Stick the steps carefully onto the balancing newel. Use balsa cement as it sets quickly. As each step sets, turn the newel and proceed.

Unit 10: Making presentation models | 53

23. SPIRAL STAIRCASES Cut a bird mouth to allow for the newel.

24. Hold the newel horizontally on the jig with double-sided tape, and stick the steps carefully onto the newel.

25. As each step sets, turn the newel and proceed.

THREE-DIMENSIONAL CURVES
Spheres and three-dimensional elements are difficult to make, so it is best to search for ready-made shapes. There are specialist suppliers for the model industry, and some professional workshops will make pieces to order for a fee. Alternatively, create a piece by making a solid core of plaster of the shape, painting it with a release agent (such as oil) covering with layers of tissue paper soaked in glue. You can also use glass fiber-reinforced resin.

TREES, ROCKS, AND WATER
Trees can be spun from wire. Cork bark can be bought from florists to make very convincing cliffs and rocks. Any shiny surface—for example, glossy paper or acrylic sheet—can represent water. The darker the material, the better the reflection. Remember, water seldom looks blue unless it is a very sunny day.

66 | Design realization

CASE STUDY 04: Updating the dated

THE BRIEF
To update a bathroom by redesigning and enlarging the interior to create a practical space that is a haven of aesthetic luxury.
Budget: Small. The client is a young professional looking for the "wow factor."
Designers: Forster, Inc.

From time to time, an interior space can lose its true purpose, becoming less efficient and less sympathetic to lifestyle requirements. In the following case study a tired and dated bathroom is redesigned and brought back to life and in the process creates a new "wow factor" for the home. Exciting design features and cutting-edge materials come together to create and transform a practical bathroom into a haven of luxury and light.

PENTHOUSE BATHROOM
All too often, practical spaces are approached with a lack of imagination and aesthetic inventiveness. This penthouse bathroom illustrates that a functional space can be entirely practical while forming a dramatic focal point within the home. The existing bathroom was too small, so the designers decided to extend the space into a hallway. The creation of a curved wall enabled them to make more efficient use of the space and doubled as an exciting design feature for the entrance to the apartment. Despite a small budget, the design team was able to create a complete transformation for the whole residence.

INDIVIDUALITY
Creating a special design feature shows innovation and individuality as well as being a highly practical design solution tailored for the user. The curved wall is made from a curved stainless steel frame, which supports a double skin of transparent acrylic.

Case study 04: Updating the dated | 67

MATERIALS AND FINISHES
Using state-of-the-art materials and clever lighting effects enabled the designers to test their ideas with new technologies while working with a team of specialized engineers. The curved wall was constructed from a laser-cut stainless steel frame, with a double layer of translucent polypropylene. Made in several pieces, the wall was delivered via the elevator and assembled on site. Colored film panels provide a contrast to the mosaic floor, while the wall is lit by a dimmable neon bulb at the base. A stainless steel cover is a clever detail used to conceal the bath pipes. The final effect achieves a new concept for the "bathroom" by replacing it with a translucent skin that glows day and night.

As the client remarks, "When you're lying in the bath, you feel like you are surrounded by a halo. The light radiates through the oranges and the reds of the acrylic wall and the whole bathroom simply glows."

METALLIC DETAILS
Smooth and shiny accents of metal are present in fixtures and fittings. A stainless steel detail provides a neat finish to conceal bath pipes.

COLOR INTERACTION
Cool blue walls and a pale blue mosaic floor set off the warm curve of the wall, creating subtle color contrasts and harmonies.

FLOATING COLOR
Orange and yellow fields of color float within the acrylic wall to create an ambient and luxurious effect from within the bathing space.

PROFESSIONAL EXAMPLES
There are plenty of professional examples of finished commissions and works in progress, with accompanying tips and insights into how to bring your work up to the highest standard.

RESOURCES
Turn to the back of the book for a glossary and useful resources, including details of colleges that provide professional qualifications.

1 Concept development

This chapter guides you through the stages of researching and developing an idea, then reviewing your idea within a context. The units in this section explore the ways in which familiar subject matter can provide an invaluable resource for study. By using observation as a tool, you will learn to draw upon your immediate environment, finding inspiration for design concepts. A range of freehand techniques—including drawing, collage, photography, and model making—will enable you to investigate form, light, texture, and scale.

Key skills in this unit are observation and research. By integrating your ideas with your own personal research, you will learn to develop a working sketchbook, explore a spatial idea, and begin to understand the design process.

See also
Unit 17: **Building components** (page 84)
Unit 18: **Building materials** (page 90)

Unit 01 : Site research and building study

OBJECTIVES
- Learn to develop a thorough study
- Provide sketches and detailed drawings
- Show use of a range of drawing materials

The starting point for any investigation is research. Whether the subject is a building, a designer, or a particular area of interest, research gives you a context within which to work and better your understanding. Research allows you to be thorough, to increase your knowledge, and to use methods and processes that lead you to make discoveries as well as solve problems. This unit will introduce the first key steps of site research and building study. The skills that you acquire will enable you to observe, question, record, and communicate architectural ideas of interest.

CAPTURING MOOD
Initial drawings can help to capture the nature of a site. Repeated heavy pencil marks build up a dramatic profile of the site.

Before you embark on designing your own ideas, it is important to have an understanding of your immediate environment. Your own likes and dislikes are often generated and shaped by the experiences around you. Until now, you may have experienced your environment as a backdrop or as busy wallpaper set against everyday routine. Now take time to notice the wealth of exciting design ideas that surround you. Site research opens you up to a world of observation. Buildings, like people, can embody personalities, values, qualities, beliefs, and ideas. Experiencing architecture means exploring and tapping into these qualities.

THE PROJECT

Choose a building that you find interesting and can easily access. Before you start drawing, take time to consider the geometry of the building. Begin by studying its form, scale, proportions, details, materials, and functions. Remember that the building itself started off as a drawing—this will help you to visualize it as a collection of horizontal and vertical planes. Use a camera to record different views, as well as close-up details and materials. Try to capture the essence and feel of the building and focus on what you wish to explore. To help develop your study, ask yourself this question: what's important?

The process

Use the architectural checklist on the right to break down your study. Once you begin drawing, try to vary the time you take to make your sketches. Timed sketches allow you to produce different types of drawings. A five-minute sketch is expressive and lively, for example, recording only important ideas and features. Use materials such as charcoal and soft pencils for speedy mark making. An accurate drawing takes more time and can provide more detailed information. The latter can be made with harder pencils for line control or ink for detailing.

Site considerations

Survey the context within which the building stands. The immediate area around your chosen site will provide you with valuable information. Create your own checklist of questions to identify important site forces. Look at the way in which the building is positioned within the street. Does it sit in a good relation to the other buildings? Is it sensitive to the surrounding architecture and, if so, how? Does it work and function well? Are there any other interesting features that may affect the way in which the building is perceived or experienced? This could be the relationship of the building to other site factors, such as a busy road, a river, a park, or a market.

AERIAL PERSPECTIVE

Aerial views of a public site establish the relationship between the building and its surrounding context. Public and private spaces are depicted with color and with arrows showing public circulation.

CHECKLIST

Solids and cavities Study the geometry of the whole building, including facades, doors, and window openings

Scale and proportion Study the scale and proportion within the building as well as its relation to the surrounding area

Rhythm Look for repetitions, ornamental details, or any lines that might suggest movement or rhythm

Texture Explore the use of materials and the contrasts that these might suggest

Light and shade Patterns of light on the building may enhance or change design elements, so look for drama

Color Explore the use of color and its effect within the building

RIVER SITE

A site near a river provides information about views, as well as describing the importance of architecture as monument or landmark within the urban landscape.

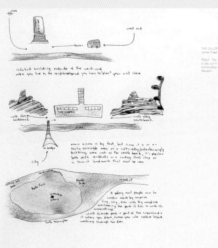

Community = All the people living in one district. The public, society

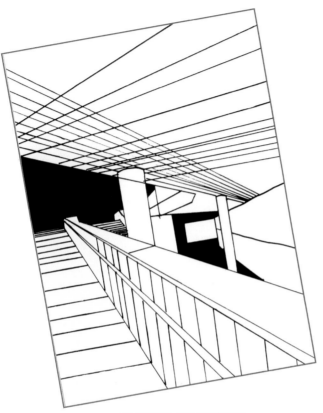

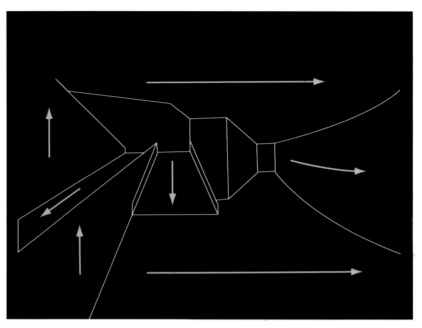

DRAWINGS AND DIAGRAMS
A diagram uses a purely visual language to communicate an idea. **Above right**, architectural elements are depicted together with arrows to describe a spatial journey. **Above**, a simple line drawing gives a perspective view of an interior site. Diminishing angles and planes create a contrast between white solid and black void.

Buildings are compositions incorporating different elements. The weave of material relationships, structures, and forms can be too overwhelming and complex to understand at first glance. The public face of buildings can inspire questions about their interior spaces. A facade that makes a bold statement may carry its design language through to inform the interior spaces within. When approaching site research, your main tool is observation. Make a checklist to help you to break down your study and focus your observation of architectural features and details into manageable stages. Whether you choose to study historical buildings such as gothic churches and classical temples, or are drawn to the design of modern buildings such as power stations or tower blocks, your study should use the prompts in the checklist to generate ideas.

OBSERVATIONAL DRAWINGS
A familiar view of the street can be the starting point for acquiring observational and drawing skills.

THE APARTMENT	THE SISTER	THE BROTHER
open welcoming adaptable	reality intuition experience	chance solitude distance

1 STRUCTURE + 2 PEOPLE = RESIDENTIAL SPACE

This project discusses the coexistence of three sets of energies in one space. Travelling and movement are the central themes. The clients are *priviledged nomads* and their conception of what a house should feel like, is equally transient.

The brother and sister share this apartment and each occupy it alternately throughout the year, and in doing so, make the best use of this costly and beautifully located apartment in central London.

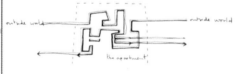

his entrance   her entrance

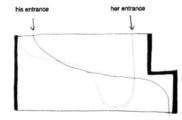

NOTES AND DIAGRAMS
Make a list of notes in your sketchbook using the prompts in the checklist on page 13 and include photographs to illustrate your text. Your research should now have provided you with photographs, sketches, diagrams, and written notes.

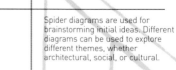

fewer possessions

if there is one home, it will
be empty for long periods
waste of space!

the home has no
fixed location

PRIVILEDGED
NOMADISM

used to constant travel

a lifestyle choice
made to match the
moment in life

in the mind of the client
there is infinite space

Spider diagrams are used for brainstorming initial ideas. Different diagrams can be used to explore different themes, whether architectural, social, or cultural.

See also
Unit 08: **Survey and freehand drawing** (page 44)

Unit 02: Building a sketchbook

OBJECTIVES
- Learn to develop ideas in a sketchbook
- Learn to develop your research in stages
- Learn to collate different pieces of information

A sketchbook is both a personal and unique journal and an invaluable archive of your ideas and mental processes. It indicates how you work, and allows you to bring together important influences and references when thinking and expressing your ideas. This unit will illustrate the importance of using a sketchbook, not as a formal presentation tool, but as a working book that helps you progress with your study.

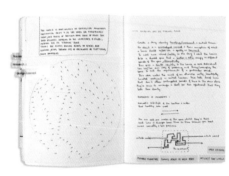

HOW TO SKETCH
Vary your methods in order to maximize the effectiveness of your sketchbook. Be adventurous and don't be too restrained—a sketchbook is a work in progress, not a final product.

Sketchbooks are vital when exploring ideas. They contain your first thoughts, allow you to glimpse possibilities when approaching a brief, and help you to work out design ideas and record what inspires and stimulates you. The sketchbook is therefore a personal journal of the steps you take in your project. These initial ideas are your starting point but may be utilized at any stage of the design process. There are no rules for compiling a working sketchbook—and there is no "right" or "wrong." Avoid being too critical at the outset and let your ideas flow freely. You will be surprised how much you can learn if you do not worry about making mistakes.

USING A SKETCHBOOK
You should use your sketchbook in a practical way to test ideas, to work out processes and methods, to record and archive research data, and to make decisions in the design process. Collect reference imagery, articles, design case studies, and photographs. Record and store them in the book in chronological order to establish a method of working. Get into the habit of making notes; this will encourage you to respond to your references. Once your ideas are informed by your research, the work you produce will be more proactive and forward-thinking.

SKETCHBOOKS AS ARCHIVES
Use a sketchbook for each project to collate design references and visual imagery that correspond to your project research. This will help to archive relevant ideas, inform design processes, and develop your design.

SPATIAL DIAGRAMS AND SKETCHES

Constant drawing and sketching will help you develop initial design ideas in response to a brief or design discussion. In the first instance, explore your ideas with diagrams. These can be effective for idea generation and are a good preparation for sketch modeling.

REFERENCES

Record your references in detail and expand these with personal notes. You may want to develop your ideas around a particular reference. Using a model or strategy is an effective way of solving a design problem or interacting with relevant issues.

ILLUSTRATIONS

Work closely with images to provoke ideas. Depicting a mood or an atmosphere early on will help you to make decisions in your design process. Use found images or create your own collages to explore instant relationships. Keep yourself inspired and stimulated with visual examples of the qualities you want to communicate.

DESIGN CRITERIA

Before long, you will have built up a set of design criteria. These are important ideas and qualities that are essential to your design processes. Try to emphasize these when making decisions about your design. They will help you to prioritize important ideas, as well as keeping you on the right track.

FOCUS ON ARCHITECTURAL FEATURES

Explore and develop ideas of architectural interest. Strong features within a space provide a good starting point for the brief.

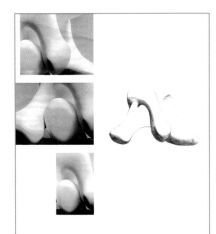

AESTHETIC INSPIRATION

Sculptural images can inspire and inform ergonomic principles and can also create a formal aesthetic for design ideas.

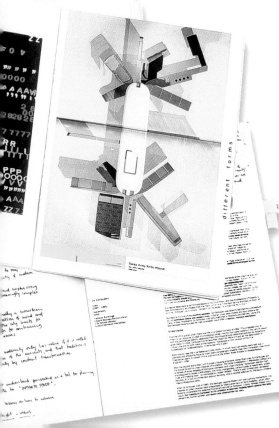

DESIGN ACCIDENTS

Trial and error is the best way of finding answers. Do not feel discouraged if you make mistakes—remember that you can only be creative if you are prepared to take risks. A fortunate discovery or a happy accident may help you realize that problems can be allies.

MAKING COLLAGES
Layer images and create collages to emphasize design ideas. Collages are a great way of exploring texture and color in combination with your ideas and images.

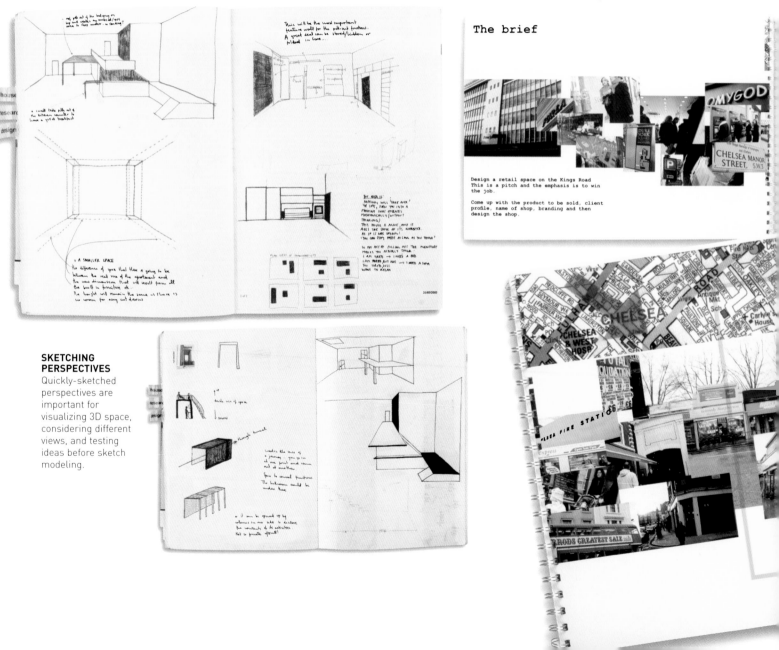

SKETCHING PERSPECTIVES
Quickly-sketched perspectives are important for visualizing 3D space, considering different views, and testing ideas before sketch modeling.

THE PROJECT

Compile the research you generated in Unit 01, including your photographs, drawings, and notes. You are now ready to explore your site research and building study by incorporating these into a sketchbook.

The process

Your investigation is set to introduce you to the beginnings of the design process. By studying the design of a building, you will now work backward to find the essence of the idea or the concept. Now that you have enough material to work with, you can begin to be playful.

STAGE 1

Choose the drawings and sketches that you feel best communicate your site research. Consider the composition of the relationships you have observed by exploring junctions: look at the ways in which materials meet, and how structural elements such as windows, doors, and stairs are organized. Take photocopies of your drawings and enlarge details. These fragments can encapsulate the idea.

STAGE 2

Now deconstruct these by breaking the geometry down to its bare minimum, pulling away layers until you reach only a few lines or planes. Combine details and fragments to create new drawings. Use your photographs in the same way and trace over them to extract ideas. Enlarge your drawings and collage into them to express materials, textures, and color. Be bold with your ideas and try to use as many different materials as you can to depict shape, form, and texture.

PLAYING WITH YOUR IDEAS

A window facade is deconstructed into a series of bold spatial geometries. Each distortion is explored with drawings (top row), diagrams (middle row), and sketch models (bottom row).

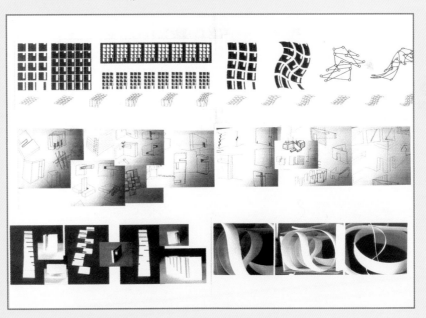

Unit 03: Making a sketch model

OBJECTIVES
- Learn to model a spatial idea
- Use a range of materials
- Use a range of modeling equipment

If you can model your ideas, you can really see what's going on in your design scheme. Materials, light, and texture make your ideas come alive in an instant and give you the opportunity to explore and reflect upon crucial design elements. Sketch models offer a real opportunity to be expressive, creative, and inventive. By using simple techniques, basic modeling tools, and inexpensive materials, you can recreate a spatial idea to scale and experience what your interior might feel like. In this unit, you will be introduced to essential skills in the processes of making sketch models to help you to develop a spatial idea.

Working with models can give you an insight into the properties of materials. Whether your design encompasses hard or soft materials, curved or angular forms, you will find out how to achieve your design ideas in the making process. Sketch modeling allows you to quickly engage with your intention, making your idea central to your choice of medium. At this stage, perfect finishes or realistic-looking models are not important; you are more concerned with using the model as a tool to find out what's possible and discover how to develop your idea spatially. Sketch modeling, by its very nature, allows things to remain loose and ambiguous, so that you can enjoy testing ideas, experimenting with different materials, and exploring the possibilities.

BASIC TOOLS
The cutting mat, utility knife, and scalpel are the basic model-making tools. Always keep a stock of extra blades to replace old ones when they become dull.

EQUIPMENT
Before you start making your sketch model you will need to gather together the right equipment. Understanding how to use your tools will help you to make effective models while using safe practices and avoiding personal injury.

Knives
For heavy-duty cutting you will need a matte knife or utility knife. This has a sturdy metal handle and ensures safety when cutting through thick or tough board. Use the straight blade for cutting cardboard, foam board, wood, and sheet metal. Use a special plastic-cutting blade for scoring and then cutting acrylics and plastics. In addition to this knife, you will also require a scalpel. This is a lightweight knife that is extremely sharp, giving accuracy and precision. It is ideal for cutting curves and small details.

Cutting mat
A cutting mat provides an effective surface on which to place all materials that need to be cut. It protects the surface of your table and helps to make cutting safe.

Rulers and squares are tools that aid adjustment and alignment; glue and pins are used for attachment and construction.

Rulers and squares

The steel ruler is the primary cutting edge. Before using the ruler, it is a good idea to give it a backing of masking tape. This helps to make the ruler non-slip when applying pressure during cutting. An engineering or "T" square is used for making right-angled cuts and for leveling models for accurate assembly.

Glue and pins

White PVA glue is used to attach most papers and cards edge to face. It is extremely effective, since it dries strong and clear. For attaching wood to wood, use PVA or balsa cement. For attaching acrylic to acrylic, use a specialized acrylic solvent. A hot glue gun can prove useful when assembling difficult-to-glue materials, such as metal, although the gun can be messy and is only suitable for sketch modeling, not for final presentation models. Spray glue is good for construction paper prior to cutting, but ensure that spray glues are used in a well-ventilated area to avoid inhalation. Use straight pins for assembling quick card models, or for supporting joints while the glue is setting.

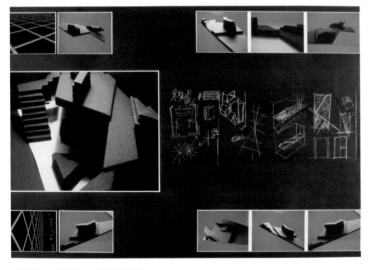

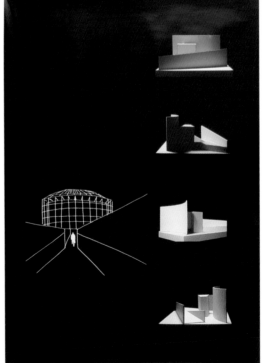

VIEWING SKETCH MODELS
Four photographs show different views of the model. Model images recreate their sculptural profiles on a black background, depicting movement with each view.

ARCHITECTURAL FRAGMENTS

A series of sketch models develops and builds ideas around an architectural fragment. Initially made in several pieces, these are then brought together in a final model. Sketches are presented together with photographs of the models to illustrate the design process.

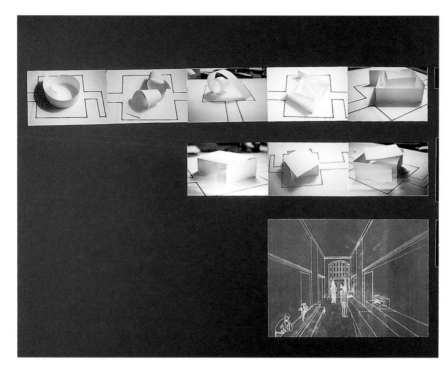

SHOWING THE PROCESS

Sketch models can be presented in sequence to communicate the process of concept development (left and below).

PRESENTING YOUR MODEL

A three-dimensional drawing shows the overall design and is presented together with the photographs of the model to illustrate the feel of the space (below).

MATERIALS

Most models can be made with basic materials, ranging from paper to heavyweight card, but beyond these, models can include an endless array of materials. Be experimental and push your ideas to the limit—the modeling process is an excellent way of gaining insight into basic construction techniques.

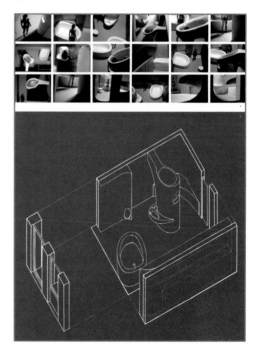

BASIC MATERIALS

Try folding, slitting, or curling simple card or paper to make quick three-dimensional sketches without using glue.

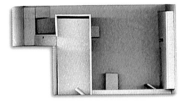

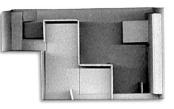

BUILDING YOUR MODEL
Photograph your model as you build it so that you have a record of each experimental design decision.

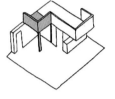

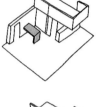

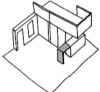

HIGHLIGHTING FEATURES
Coloring different elements of your sketch can highlight specific features of your model to which you want to draw attention.

THE PROJECT

Using the material you have already generated in your sketchbook from Unit 2, select one architectural fragment from your building study. Study this fragment and decide what materials it can be made from. Try to choose a material that will evoke the properties and qualities this fragment suggests. At right, an image of refracted light is developed into an idea for a walkway. The materials used in the model explore contrasts between transparent and opaque surfaces.

The process

You can use card stock, foam board, wire, tracing paper, sheet metal, acrylic, or balsa wood for building structure. Experiment with different techniques, such as twisting, rolling, tearing, scoring, or folding card stock to create junctions and planes. For more defined meeting points, use glue to attach one material to another. Remember to consider the scale of the drawing and try to respond to material relationships by keeping these proportions consistent. Make a series of three or four sketch models, all exploring one fragment. Try to differentiate these by testing various options— contrast materials, colors, textures, and effects.

STAGE 1

Choose a material that best suits your idea. Consider how to use it to construct the main body of your fragment. Begin by making a simple framework.

STAGE 2

Now apply other materials and textures to build up this structure. These can be elements that are attached, clad, or slotted into your structure, depending on the relationship you wish to explore and the detail you want to represent.

STAGE 3

Analyze what you have made. Does your spatial model clearly capture your fragment? Build upon what you have made so far by revising and adjusting elements that can be improved.

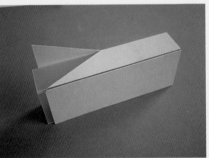

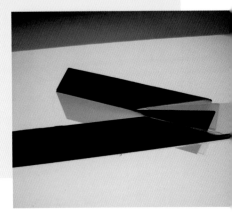

Unit 04: Developing an idea

See also

Unit 01: **Site research and building study** (page 12)
Unit 07: **Architectural drawing conventions** (page 40)
Unit 13: **Creating a brief** (page 70)

OBJECTIVES
- Learn to research an initial idea and develop a concept board
- Build your understanding of design criteria
- Explore methods of communicating ideas in 2D and 3D

The beginning of any project may seem daunting—with so many different possibilities and decisions, how do you go about choosing an idea? The first important stage of the process is to enjoy the possibilities, and be inspired by the process. It is crucial that you remain open-minded and avoid making final decisions about the design. The more material you have to choose from, the more interesting your decision-making will be. In this unit, you will learn how to gather initial ideas together to help you develop a concept board.

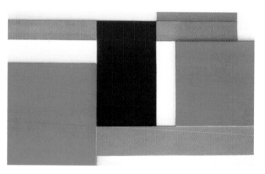

BASIC SHAPES
A landscape image **(top)** provides inspiration for initial ideas. It is abstracted into a series of horizontal and vertical planes **(above)** to explore spatial geometries.

FINDING AN IDEA

Inspiration has no boundaries and can come from a variety of sources. You can develop your ideas from a painting, a piece of writing, an object, an image, or even an evocative memory. At this stage, you should keep your process open and your thinking as creative as possible. This means working quickly, being intuitive, and recording your initial responses to the brief. This conceptual level of the project allows you to express yourself without focusing on the individual element or details. It is a more general way of operating, in which you work up the design concept as a whole to enable a cohesive scheme to emerge. At this stage, your work will consist of gathering information, identifying interests, generating ideas, carrying out relevant research, and considering your brief.

DEVELOPING THE IDEA

Once you have established an area of interest, focus on specific ideas. This second stage allows you to move your analysis from the whole to its parts. Collate visual references and make notes. Keep a sketchbook to record your process—this is an invaluable reference book, which can help you later in the design development stages. Analyze what you have—what are the issues, values, qualities, and elements? Are they physical, conceptual, spatial, or historical?

These ideas can be tested in a series of sketch models. Remember these are not intended to be functional—sketch models should try to express an idea spatially. They can resemble spatial diagrams, moving the idea away from two dimensions. At this stage, your work should be engaged with questioning and deconstructing ideas, developing responses to the brief, testing ideas with spatial models, considering important design criteria, and contemplating alternative possibilities.

A response to:
Vision

conceal
reveal
reflect
shade
view
line of sight
transparent
distort

EXPLORING THE CONTEXT
Study views and vistas to develop and explore the relationship between the users and their environment.

TEST POSSIBILITIES
Provide a series of planning diagrams before choosing a final scheme.

CONSIDERING DETAILS
Sculpture and installation images are good references that depict material qualities as well as spatial narratives.

MAKING A CONCEPT BOARD

Once you have a sketchbook of ideas and a sketch model, you are ready to present the first stage of the project to the client. The presentation should be professional standard, with neat, crisp work and well kept models. Concept boards are an excellent way of communicating the general level of the idea and introducing some design ideas for the scheme. You can also compile your sketches, photographs, and site research into a spiral-bound document, together with your intended design proposal. At this stage you are ready to make design decisions, though these are not final and may further develop and change with the later stages of the project. Your work should focus on collating ideas for presentation, show initial design decisions, and provide an initial design proposal by illustrating important ideas on a concept board.

THE PROJECT

Choose five words. Make sure that they are words that you find sufficiently interesting to work with. Look up their true meanings in the dictionary. Keep these in your project book. You may find it helpful to brainstorm with these words. See what other ideas they may suggest to you and, in particular, focus on the qualities they project.

The process

Collect images that represent these words. You may have to categorize these into specific or abstract, architectural or atmospheric, illustrative or reference imagery. Deconstruct these images by selecting specific ideas that you wish to explore and use these as a resource for developing your sketch models. Create a size C (17" x 22") or international A2 size (16.54" x 23.39") concept board, using the images you have sourced together with your chosen words.

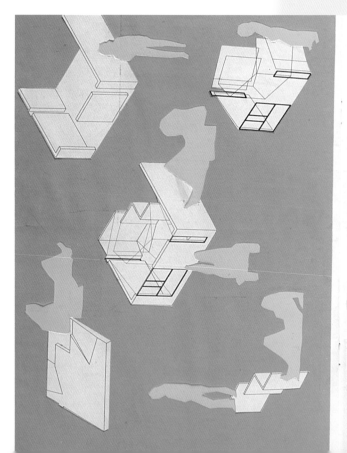

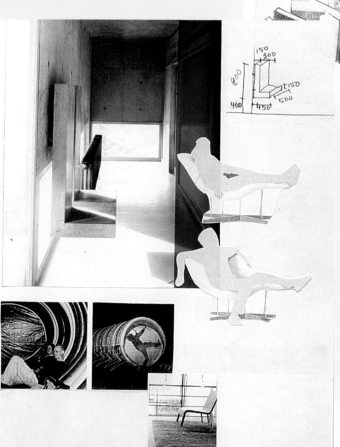

CONCEPT BOARDS
Here, a grid of abstract images and words are juxtaposed to create immediate narratives for the viewer.

STAGE 1

Begin by brainstorming, responding quickly and intuitively to any associations and ideas that your chosen words suggest. There will be obvious qualities as well as some subtle ones that are not readily perceived. Record these in a simple and visual spider diagram, showing how words and ideas are related and connected.

STAGE 2

Define these words with specific images. Try to communicate and represent these words visually. Include any other words that have emerged from the brainstorming exercise and that you feel are important in order to expand and give texture to your initial ideas.

STAGE 3

Juxtapose your final selection of words and images on your concept board. Consider the relationship between images and text to make the most effective presentation. Explore the grouping of images and play with the layout before you glue the elements down. Once you are happy with the composition, use spray glue to carefully mount all the material, finalizing your concept board.

STAGE 4

Present your concept board to a friend or colleague for feedback. This is an important exercise, since it will allow you to gauge the effectiveness of your concept board. Always be prepared to take constructive criticism; it is a vital part of developing your practice.

CASE STUDY 01: Modern restaurant

THE BRIEF
Redesign an existing space to accommodate a modern Italian restaurant for 48 diners.
Budget: Good to moderate.
The client has stressed that the food is the most important factor—everything else is secondary.
Designers: ARTEC

Interior designers are often called upon to modify and improve existing spaces, either by reorganizing what already exists, or by providing entirely new programs and functions for space. The following case study illustrates an intended concept and proposal for a restaurant based in a busy metropolitan environment. Faced with an empty shell, the design team must build an entire scheme that defines the building's function and creates the ambience required for relaxed dining.

A sense of space, light, texture, and easy Mediterranean living are evoked by the juxtaposition of imagery and use of color.

STAGE 1 Brainstorming
At the preliminary meeting the design team was able to draw inspiration from the client's passion for food and generate the initial concept ideas. The approach to the brief was kept simple. Signature dishes from the menu were used as inspiration and to suggest and identify the qualities of the envisaged restaurant setting. By transposing these qualities into words, the team were able to inspire interior ideas and images based around the theme of "modern rustic."

STAGE 2 Communicating the concept
The designer collected images that represent the key words, and a concept board was presented to the client to help visualize the potential scheme by suggesting materials, physical relationships, spatial qualities, and atmosphere.

A key design consideration was that the interior should complement the food without being too prominent. This means that subtle material contrasts need to be achieved using natural materials such as slate and stone for practical areas and wood for dining areas. The interior can then be further controlled by the use of ambient lighting.

KEY WORDS:

FARMHOUSE   WARM   MODERN
RUSTIC.   INTIMATE   BALANCED
SIMPLE   EARTHY   STYLE
HONEST   COZY   CLEAN

PUTTING IT INTO WORDS
Beginning with a simple concept, the designer began by brainstorming with words to help inspire interior ideas and images.

CONCEPT BOARD
Images can be specific or abstract, architectural or atmospheric. The designer has collated photographs and tearsheets from magazines and suppliers' catalogs to evoke the feel of the scheme.

While not intended as a materials sample board, it includes images of lighting fittings that may potentially be used in the final design.

Mood lighting will be a major feature of this scheme, so it features strongly here.

SECTION DRAWING
A section drawing (right) shows the array of different materials used in a washroom space.

SKETCH PERSPECTIVE
This is a freehand line drawing, rapidly sketched on site. It communicates the idea of the layout economically, but doesn't really convey atmosphere and detail.

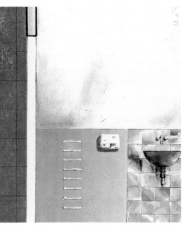

SAMPLE MATERIALS
Along with the perspective drawings, these allow the client to visualize how the scheme will really look.

RENDERED PERSPECTIVE
This is drawn to scale (right), and provides real detail of materials, furniture, and lighting to give a sense of the overall ambience of the interior.

STAGE 5 Floor plan

In any project the floor plan is the most important drawing. It shows the complete layout of the scheme, including the position of furniture, entrances, exits, light sources, and circulation areas. A restaurant is a functional environment, and the design should not lose sight of these practicalities.

Though minor changes might occur, this stage usually signifies an agreement has been reached between client and designer with regard to the final design.

STAGE 3 Preliminary sketch

Different drawings can help identify the different stages of a design process. Freehand drawings are usually used at the start of the project for a "pitch presentation" to the client. At this stage the designer is not getting paid, and so works quickly to win the sale.

A sketch perspective is characterized by its loose and energetic style and helps the client to visualize the reality and the energy of initial ideas. Although these ideas may change, they provide an important starting point for a discussion of what the design proposal should include.

STAGE 4 Presentation perspective

There is no doubt that a real-life depiction of the scheme helps clinch the deal between designer and client. Every client wants to know what they're getting, and a presentation drawing strives to seduce them by communicating the look of the final design. Unlike the sketch perspective, it is rendered to scale and provides more substantial information about the design scheme.

FLOOR LAYOUT
Computer-aided design gives clarity to this scale image of the restaurant floor plan.

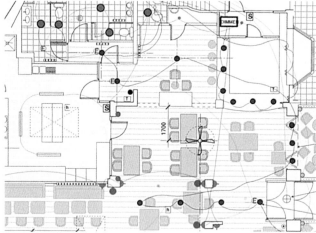

CASE STUDY 02: Interior to exterior

THE BRIEF
To create a new "diner" style space, with doors opening onto a garden.
Budget: Small. The clients are a professional couple with a shared interest in 1930's and 1950's interior products and architecture.
Designers: Fieldhouse Associates

The journey from interior to exterior often crosses an exciting threshold, which must be considered by the designer. It is essential for any design scheme to explore how the interior and exterior worlds meet, and when the inside space is intended to flow and encompass an outdoor space. In this case study, the importance of a garden view dominates the design of an extension and in doing so creates a new living space within a family home.

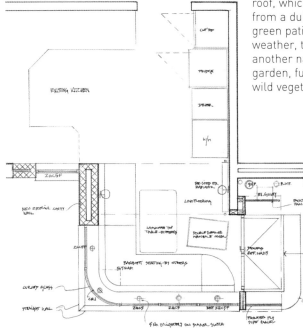

Copper materials on the roof add natural textures to the garden, blending in with plants and foliage to inspire outdoor relaxation.

DESIGNING WITH STYLE
Residential design often draws inspiration from the lifestyle requirements and cultural interests of the client. This kitchen extension within a 19th-century terraced house began with style as its starting point. The clients were eager to evoke the feel of a "diner" style of dining bay by connecting the kitchen and dining area to the garden. The designer was able to use historical Art Deco references to help create a streamlined structure. Using a steel-framed curved glass window, a wrap-around structure was created. This formed the basis of the seating area inside, while keeping the exterior sympathetic with the existing planting outside.

DESIGN CONSTRUCTION
This micro building sports a copper roof, which in time will be transformed from a dull brown color to a lustrous green patination. By responding to the weather, the roof structure becomes another natural element within the garden, further echoing the rich and wild vegetation.

Up close, the curve of the bay window reveals myriad design details, which help to enhance this wrap-around structure.

THE PLAN
The plan provides a comprehensive overview of the layout and arrangement of the new extension. Functional areas, such as the kitchen, and the position of appliances are kept separate with good planning and circulation for domestic ease. The relaxation areas, freed from utility, are given the garden views.

The bespoke banquette seating picks up references to art deco styles with its ambient use of muted leather and its curved and streamlined shape.

Maximum light sources connect the garden to the interior space, making light and view a dramatic feature of the space.

INTERIOR FURNITURE

The use of clean curved lines and muted colors continues the language of the exterior into the interior. Custom-built banquette seating describes the curved shape of the bay window and utilizes the design for maximum dining space. Materials play an important role, with soft leather upholstery for comfort and shiny aluminum details which provide both contrast and accents of light.

2 Design realization

Design realization continues the design process with an introduction to basic freehand and orthographic drawing techniques. This chapter teaches you how to record information on an initial site visit, and how to develop a freehand drawing into a technically constructed plan, section, and three-dimensional view of the interior. From technical equipment to drawing techniques, the design principles taught in this chapter will provide the necessary skills for proceeding with the advanced development stages of a design scheme.

Key skills covered in this chapter include numeracy, scale, proportion, technical drawing, presentation, and communication skills.

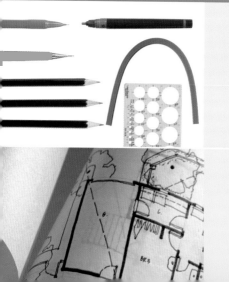

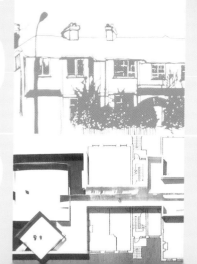

Unit 05: Drawing materials

OBJECTIVES
- Introduce a range of drawing materials
- Introduce a range of graphic techniques
- Develop your understanding of design drawings

A good range of graphic tools will enable you to communicate the subtleties of your design. Along with practicing and developing your own drawing style, you need to develop an understanding of when and where a particular graphic technique might be effectively employed. This unit will introduce you to a variety of drawing materials that may inspire you to produce quality drawings.

Drawing equipment is used to produce a design drawing and communicate the idea behind it. Whether you are drafting in pencil or ink, you will need to employ a range of graphic techniques, either to represent a variety of soft or hard materials and geometric shapes, or simply to indicate a pitch in a roof or the angle of a stair. The first step is to bring together the equipment that you will need in order to practice your drawing techniques.

Lead holder pencil

Mechanical clutch pencil

Paper

Wooden lead pencils

PAPER
Typo detail paper is used for sketching, planning, layouts, and survey notes. This is a relatively inexpensive alternative to tracing paper with good transparency for overlaying drawings. Tracing paper is expensive and should only be used for final presentation drawings. The quality of tracing paper varies according to its weight with a high-quality weight being about 42 lbs. and a good general-purpose weight being about 28 lbs.

WOODEN LEAD PENCIL
An ordinary lead pencil made from wood is generally good for sketching, freehand drawing, or planning layouts. You can sharpen this with a pencil sharpener, but a blade will give a better line quality. Wooden lead pencils can vary in lead weight to give different degrees of hardness. Use 4H or 2H leads to provide you with more control when drawing hard to medium-hard accurate lines. A good general-purpose lead weight is an F or H, which is

used for finished drawings, accurate layouts, and lettering, whereas a soft pencil, such as an HB, allows for bold line work but requires much more control, and the lead can smear during drafting.

LEAD HOLDER PENCIL
The use of this pencil requires much more skill and experience, as it is able to make a variety of line weights. Always ensure that the lead is sharpened so that it has a long taper. Practice by pulling the line and rotating the pencil at the same time to achieve an accurate line quality. Remember always to pull your line up (bottom to top) or across (left to right) and never push a line. If you push the pencil, you may put too much pressure on it, either breaking the lead or ruining the page.

MECHANICAL CLUTCH PENCIL
These pencils are designed to produce a consistent line—0.5 mm, for example—and therefore do not require sharpening. For bold and dense lines you can double up the line or alternatively use 0.3 mm, 0.7 mm, and 0.9 mm leads to vary your line weights. The mechanical clutch pencil is the easiest pencil to use because it gives you more control than the other types. Be careful not to drop your pencil, as the lead tends to break easily.

Technical pens

TECHNICAL PENS

Technical pens produce accurate and precise line widths with clarity and definition. The most delicate part of the pen is the tubular metal nib, which regulates the flow of ink. Like the mechanical clutch pencil, pens can be bought in sets of different sizes, such as 0.18 mm, 0.25 mm, 0.35 mm, and 0.5 mm. When inking, you should work from left to right and from top to bottom, allowing the ink to dry as you work. Store pens nib upward.

DRAWING BOARD

All technical drawings are produced on a drawing board or drafting table to ensure accuracy. This means that your drawings will have accurately drawn lines as well as angles. The parallel motion moves up and down, allowing you to keep all the horizontal lines parallel in your drawing. Ensure that the surface of your board and your parallel motion is regularly cleaned. You can use a mild surface cleanser or lighter fluid for cleaning.

ADJUSTABLE SET SQUARE

Adjustable set square

The adjustable triangle is used to produce all vertical lines that sit at 90 degrees to the parallel motion as well as those that are pitched or sloped at other angles. A large set square, 12 in. (300 mm) and with a beveled edge, is most practical. Make sure that you do not use it as a cutting edge, as this will impair the acrylic. Keep it clean with lighter fluid.

CIRCLE TEMPLATE AND COMPASS

A circle template is extremely useful for drawing small-to-medium circles, or for drawing arches and rounded edges. A compass is used for larger circles, and is useful for ink work.

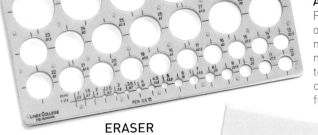
Circle template

ERASER SHIELD AND DRAFTING BRUSH

An eraser shield allows you to be precise when erasing certain areas of the drawing. It is also useful for protecting the surface of the drawing from being ruined or marred by the eraser. Try to use a soft eraser when removing a line, and use a drafting brush to keep your drawing surface clean.

Compass

Eraser shield

ERASER

A range of erasers will allow you to remove both graphite and ink. A white eraser is used to erase pencil, and the putty type is good for tidying drawings. Large areas of ink can be removed with a plastic eraser, and then scratched out with a scalpel.

SCALE RULER

A scale ruler allows you to convert true size into different scales. The most commonly used scales are 1:5, 1:10, 1:20, 1:50, and 1:100. All measurements should be given in millimeters and meters.

Eraser

FRENCH CURVES AND FLEXI CURVES

Flexi curve

For more complex curves and organic shapes, use French curves made from acrylic or flexi curves made from rubber. These can help to draw larger elements, such as a curved wall or a shapely piece of furniture.

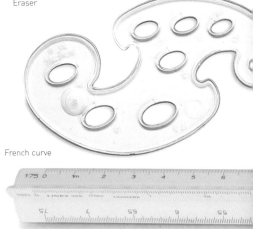
French curve

Scale ruler

See also

Unit 11: Axonometric and perspective drawings (page 54)

Unit 06: Human dimensions

OBJECTIVES
- Introduce the principles of scale and proportion
- Introduce principles of ergonomics
- Understand the importance of design data

Our sense of aesthetics comes from the human body. Human scale is the most important factor influencing human design, simply because everything that is designed specifically responds to need, and therefore has a purpose or an intention. Our bodily dimensions can determine how we feel and react within interior spaces. This unit focuses on the importance of the principles that govern our design decisions. Ergonomics, scale, and proportion are primary factors in the study of architecture and interior design.

SCALE

Measurement is a great feat of abstraction. In practical life we are rarely confronted with the need to compare height with length and breadth. While we may not know that, on average, our outstretched hands from fingertip to fingertip will span the same distance as our overall height, we do associate height with dominance. The large size or scale of an interior, an object, or another person can make us feel small or intimidated. This feeling of being either de-humanized or overawed is important to the design of certain social settings, such as tower blocks, skyscrapers, shopping malls, and churches. These can be designed with the human scale in mind either to convey power, impose authority, or simply to impress. How we perceive these qualities also depends on whether we feel the scale is appropriate to the context. In other words, we might not mind whether something is big or small if it feels right. Consequently, a designer may want to break with convention and use scale as a device to change behavior.

EVERYDAY SCALE
Everything in the environment acts as a tool by which to discern the scale of things. Telegraph poles, street lamps, trees, cars, buildings, and people help to give us an understanding of dimension, size, and proportion.

HUMANS WITHIN A SPACE
Nonstatic images (below) depict movement and circulation through an interior. Dimensions should consider movement when designing functional spaces.

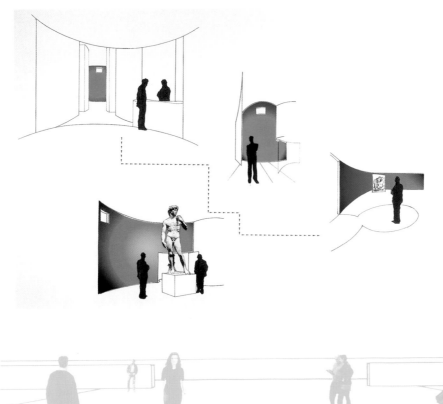

EXHIBITION INTERIOR
An exhibition space is a public interior, which has been designed to consider the scale and circulation of its artifacts and spaces. It is important that the visitor is able to see objects up close as well as from afar.

USING FIGURES
Two-dimensional drawings are flat in nature and become more three-dimensinal when figures are introduced. These not only describe scale and proportion, but can also bring depth into the picture plane by making a distinction between foreground and background.

PROPORTION
Mathematical and geometric methods have allowed designers to consider the ideal proportion of things. Proportioning moves beyond function or technical concerns to achieve harmony, balance, or unity. A proportional system establishes a consistent set of visual references. Here, scale is not important in itself; it is the ratio of one measurement or proportion to another that is important. We always experience things in relation to something else, whether this is color, texture, material, shape, or form. Our perception of proportion is useful because it allows us to enjoy or question physical and material relationships. Establishing these relationships can include creating big contrasts as well as describing subtle ones.

SCALE FIGURES
Models use scale figures to enhance their reality. A figure placed within an interior brings it to life.

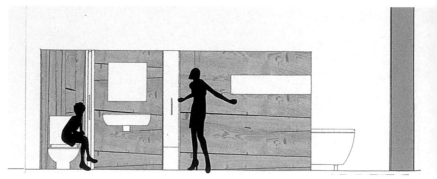

HUMAN DIMENSIONS

The human body can be thought of as a simple framework consisting of a series of basic proportions. These can be broken down into seven equal parts with the head being proportionately one-seventh of the total height. Standing eye level is given an approximate height of 5 feet (1500 mm), even though this will vary from person to person. Once a proportional system is applied to designing an interior space, this can give clarity to understanding or envisaging what the eye will experience.

A scheme that gives importance to the eye level helps to connect us physically to our immediate environment by providing views. A scheme that controls what we see, on the other hand, will further our curiosity by encouraging expectation. Whether we are static, standing, seated, or on the move, comfort and practicality can be designed for every activity.

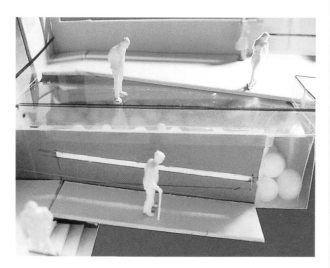

MODEL FIGURES
Presentations can take into account human dimensions by providing model figures to scale.

THE PROJECT

Test your understanding of good and bad design by considering two ergonomic objects in your home or work environment. Choose one object that you think is well designed and one that is poorly designed.

The process

Give a detailed critique of why these two objects represent examples of good and bad design. List the main reasons why each object fails or succeeds in its function, how it could be improved, and suggest the features it should or should not include. As an aspiring designer, you should develop your own opinions about good and bad design—this will help you to question your own design criteria when approaching your work.

ERGONOMICS

When something is ergonomic, it functions well and supports us within our practical environment. Ergonomic principles can be found in every practical object designed for human activity. For anything intended for human use, from cutlery to stairs, a designer should consider ease, practicality, and comfort, designing in response to need, function, or task.

The paperclip is simple and functional in design. Entirely ergonomical, it attaches documents together while remaining flat.

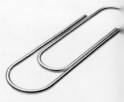

Hats can be practical, functional, and aesthetic. A hard hat is designed specifically as a safety device to protect the wearer in construction environments.

Sneakers can be made from soft or hard materials for durability, comfort, and practicality.

Spectacle frames must be ergonomic in their design in order to fit the face well.

An excellent example of compact design, the Swiss Army knife houses a series of miniature tools. It is discreet and portable for ultimate practicality.

The supermarket trolley defines retail design by being stackable while being able to hold a large volume of goods.

Board games are highly visual and graphic to communicate rules and principles for play. Game pieces are designed to be tactile for movement and for use.

A frying pan should have a heat-resistant handle and a heat-conducting body.

A suitcase must be hardwearing, able to carry heavy loads, and include latches, locks, and handles.

A cog is a simple form, following function. Made from durable materials, they are important mechanisms, found in many different machines.

A practical object used for air circulation and ventilation, a fan can be a highly aesthetic object of design.

A chair supports people in many different environments, and needs to be both functional and aesthetic in design.

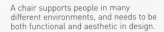

The internal compartment of a radio contains electrical circuits and wiring. Its exterior casing is often designed to suit domestic settings to cater for different consumer tastes and styles.

A guitar's strings are stretched across its hollow body to produce and amplify sound.

Unit 07: Architectural drawing conventions

OBJECTIVES
- Understand how to read a range of architectural drawings
- Understand the use of drawing conventions
- Learn to construct a technical drawing

Designers and architects all use a visual language to communicate their ideas. Just as with any other language, architectural drawings are subject to conventions—these are then translated to practically represent ideas. Technical drawings are required for both communicating and constructing a design. This unit will cover the basic principles of technical drawing needed to produce drawings suited to a client presentation.

TECHNICAL DRAWING

Architectural drawings emphasize the form and definition of space. Drawings can either be two- or three-dimensional in their graphic representation. Plans, sections, and elevations are all two-dimensional views that are collectively known as orthographic projection. Each view represents our envisioned movement around the space, while keeping the scale and proportion of dimensions consistent. The plan takes us on a journey above the space; the elevation allows us to approach the space from the outside at ground level, and the section invites us inside to observe the configuration of spaces from within. The importance of these views resides in their ability to present information in an orthographic sequence. Consequently, when the drawings are presented as a set, they provide many different layers of information, giving a comprehensive understanding of a design scheme.

Three-dimensional drawings consist of axonometrics, isometrics, and perspective drawings. These drawings are more realistic, as they allow us to see all three dimensions of height, length, and width (see page 54).

AXONOMETRIC DRAWING
This black and white axonometric drawing draws attention to the use of the light sources. A series of hatched lines on the floor describes how natural light is used for practical activities such as washing and bathing.

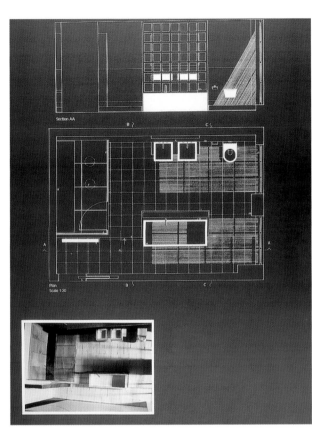

require that all section lines be drawn with the heaviest line weight to indicate the immediacy of the cut point. Although you will be expected to draw everything from the cut point through to the back of the interior, everything else that is not cut through will be indicated in a lighter line weight to give depth.

PLAN

The plan is a horizontal view of the building once it has been cut just above waist height, 4 feet (1200 mm), and the top section is removed. The purpose of the plan is to show the organization and layout of spaces within the building. The cut height is determined by the need to include important information, such as the position of doors, windows, walls, and stairs, as well as showing the thickness of structural walls, stud walls, window frames, and sills. Other important architectural features above the cut level are also included in the plan. Structural beams, mezzanines, or skylights are represented with a dotted line to indicate that they are above head and above the cut level.

PLAN AND SECTION

The plan is presented with its corresponding section above to give both aerial and vertical views of the interior. A photograph of the scale model shows the sculptural and material quality of the scheme, and the drama of light and shade.

SECTIONS AND ELEVATIONS

Sections and elevations are vertical views of the building. The elevation is used to illustrate the exterior facade of a building and therefore does not cut through the building. Details such as pillars, arches, doors, and windows can all be shown in an elevation, while the section allows us to remove this face with a vertical cut through to see the internal spaces hidden within. Section views are either long or short, depending on whether you cut through the length or width of the building. When choosing which part of the interior to illustrate in the form of a section, it is common to choose the most important view. This means providing as much information as possible, showing any level changes, double height spaces, or staircases. The section drawing is constructed directly from the plan, using light construction lines to project information such as heights and lengths or widths. The cut-through point is indicated on the outside of the plan with section arrows showing the position of the cut, as well as the direction of its view. Drawing conventions

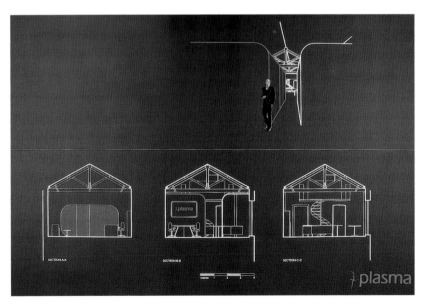

SECTIONS

Sections are important for describing the architectural features of a given site. These sections show a roof structure.

SCALE

Scale simply means size. Most technical drawings are drawn to scale, so that land, buildings, and objects are not represented at their true size, but much smaller. This enables the design drawing to fit on the page. The scales most commonly used are 1:20, 1:50, and 1:100. A drawing of an interior at scale 1:20 is 20 times smaller, or one-twentieth of the real size. This means that the real size of the interior is 20 times bigger than its representation. As the scale of the drawing increases, more detail must be shown. A scale drawing at 1:100 means that one meter measures one centimeter (or one yard measures just over a third of an inch). A scale bar is a device used to show the scale of a drawing by providing a bar that is the same scale as the drawing. It is particularly useful when drawings are photocopied and reduced to a given size rather than a given scale. Different types of scale bar are used according to your graphic style or drawing preference.

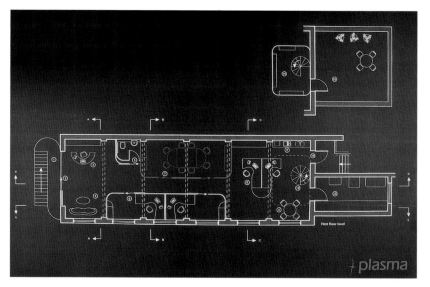

SECTION LINES

Section lines indicate the most important views within the interior and are labeled outside the plan with arrowheads showing the direction chosen.

HIGHLIGHTING A FEATURE

When offered as a package, a series of technical drawings helps to communicate the design scheme in an orthographic sequence. A computer-generated image illustrates an important seating feature central to the design concept of this domestic interior.

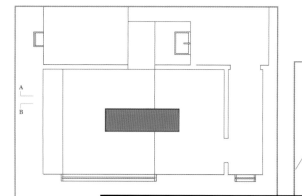

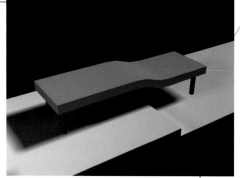

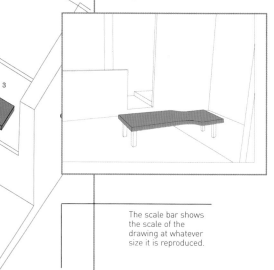

The scale bar shows the scale of the drawing at whatever size it is reproduced.

SCALE : mm
0   500   1000

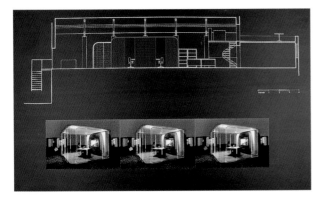

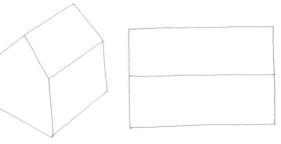

LONG SECTION
A long section describes the length of the building as opposed to its width. Section views are flat depictions of space; when presented together with other views or models they help to give a comprehensive understanding of the scheme.

THREE-DIMENSIONAL AND ROOF PLAN
Exterior views of a building are represented by vertical elevations, with an aerial view of the roof plan.

DIMENSION LINES AND SECTION LINES
These lines should be drawn with technical drawing instruments for clarity and consistency. The type of graphic representation will vary to suit the drawing and its style. Keep all dimension lines and section lines clear from the drawing to avoid confusion.

LINE WEIGHTS
The thickness of your line indicates cut-through points, structural and non-structural elements, as well as furniture and detail. Your thickest line (0.5, 0.7, 0.8, and 1.0) represents the outline, structure, or profile of the space at the cut-through point. The thicker the line, the more contrast there is between the profile of the space and the other lines used to draw furniture and details. This gives the drawing a feeling of depth.

If you have a lot of fine detail in a section, such as cornices or other architectural detailing, this may dictate the line weight used. A heavy line, if used to draw a detailed profile, could look insensitive and a lot of detail could be lost. The general rule for line weights is governed by the position of the cut-through point. The further away you move from the cut line, the lighter the line weight. Details such as tiles and floorboards will be furthest away from the cut line and should be drawn with a fine pen (0.1, 0.18) to suggest distance. Furniture and non-structural elements should be drawn with a medium line weight (0.25, 0.35) to contrast with fine detail and heavy profiles.

DOORS AND WINDOWS
Conventions for drawing doors and windows can vary. With a door, it is important to show how it is hinged, so the door is drawn to show it open at a 90-degree angle. Windows are drawn at the cut-though point, which is higher than the sill; therefore the sill is shown with a lighter line than the window frame.

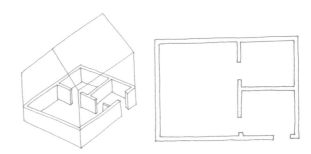

PLAN SECTION
Cut at waist height, a horizontal section through the building gives a plan view of the interior spaces.

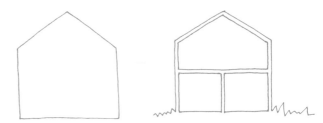

ELEVATION AND SECTION
When the elevation is cut through vertically it creates a section view of the interior spaces within the building.

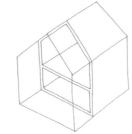

SECTIONAL ELEVATION
A sectional elevation will show elements that have been cut through, as well as others which have not. Some elements will therefore be in section, while others away from the cut line will remain in elevation.

See also
Unit 01: **Site research and building study** (page 12)

Unit 08: Survey and freehand drawing

A survey allows you to record and process the information needed to produce measured drawings. Whether you have a kitchen or a whole building to survey, the procedure is the same. By using sharp observation skills, you can record the information needed to produce accurate freehand drawings. This unit offers a step-by-step guide to surveying a space and develops your freehand drawing skills.

The initial procedure when surveying a space is to make sure you have the right equipment. You will need a long 30-yard tape measure, as well as a convenient pocket-size measure, a folding rod, a carpenter's rule for measuring pitches and angles, a ledger-size vellum paper pad, pencils, and a camera.

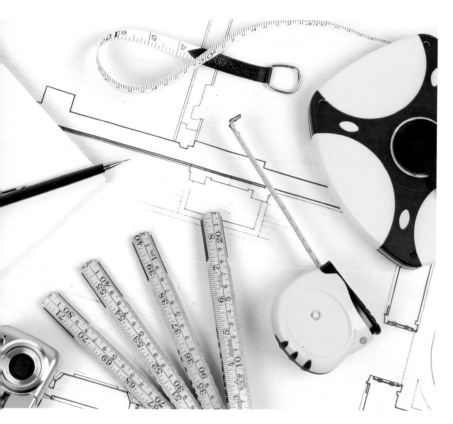

STAGE 1

Collect any available drawings or photographs. If you have a fairly big site to survey, it is a good idea to collect any existing drawings by making a request to the local city planning department, borrowing old drawings from the owner, or by researching historical records in national or local archives. This information is useful, but you will still need to take site measurements to confirm the accuracy of any drawings you obtain.

STAGE 2

Arrange to visit the building. Make sure you arrange access to the building well in advance. This will save you time and unnecessary delay when you arrive at the site. Allow for a good amount of time to survey—at least half a day—so that there is no need to return because you are short of time.

STAGE 3

Decide how you will survey and establish a program. Before you begin the physical survey, take time to walk around your site to appreciate the size, shape, and proportion of the spaces. Note anything that might

EQUIPMENT
Preparation is the key for surveying a space. Bring together your equipment and be methodical in your practice. Patience and careful observation will ensure accuracy.

obstruct measurements, such as large machinery or furniture. You may need to organize a second trip if you are unable to get all measurements on the initial visit.

STAGE 4

Prepare freehand drawings. Before you start measuring with your tape you will need a set of well-proportioned freehand plans and sections to place your measurements upon. Start by pacing out the space in order to establish the ratio of length to width. Draw these light guidelines of your plan, ignoring all detail. Pace out the position of other elements such as windows, doors, fireplaces, cabinets, steps, and radiators.

Now complete your sketch by drawing over the guidelines and situating these elements in their correct position. Any important overhead information, such as beams, should be drawn in a dotted line—the convention denotes longer dashes for information above the cut-through point and shorter dashes to indicate hidden elements below or behind elements on the plan. Carefully observe any construction and establish which walls are load-bearing and which are partition, relating any overhead beams to supporting wall projections. Show floorboard direction and indicate the north point on the plan by using a compass or a map. This will be important when considering how the light sources affect the space.

If you are surveying more than one floor, you must show how the spaces or rooms relate to one another, and how each floor level relates to the one above. Use an overlay of vellum paper over the ground floor plan as a guide to draw the layout of floors above or below. In most cases it will be possible to trace the size and positions of main architectural features, such as walls, windows, and staircases. These details must never be assumed and always checked by careful measurements. Sections are drawn using the most informative position for the imaginary cut line. In your final drawings, this position is always indicated on the plans by section arrows.

STAGE 5

Before you begin measuring, mark up your drawings with dimension lines. This saves time and ensures that you establish the dimensions you will need. Wherever possible, place dimension lines outside the plan, and when measuring running dimensions, go clockwise.

STAGE 6

Measuring is best done by two people to ensure accuracy and practicality. One person holds the zero end of the tape and writes down dimensions as the other reels out the tape, takes a measurement and calls it out, repeating it to confirm.

The main dimensions will be running dimensions. These are linear dimensions that begin from a single point, usually the corner of the room, and continue to get larger until the far corner is reached. This will give you a total length for each wall rather than a series of sums to add up, avoiding error. Use your folding ruler to measure wall recesses and your pocket measure to access detailed areas inside window openings. Establish the relative position of door and window openings and major structures such as brick piers and fireplaces using the running method before taking smaller dimensions.

If the rooms are not square, diagonal measurements must be taken from the corners in order to establish the angles of the walls. The measurements are placed against diagonal lines on the freehand plan. Always take care to note dimensions on these drawings very carefully. When using metric measurements, use millimeters and meters, not centimeters. Show the start and finish of running dimensions.

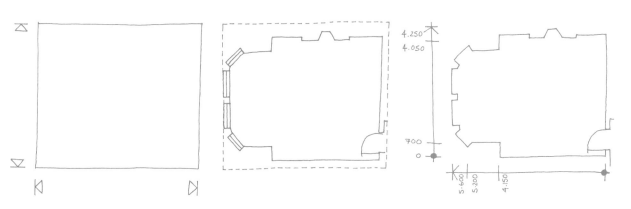

CONSTRUCTING A FREEHAND PLAN
Pacing out the dimensions of the space, make a freehand sketch and carve out the profile of the space, including the position of all existing elements, until you have an accurate plan. This is used to place all running dimensions when surveying the space.

See also
Unit 07: **Architectural drawing conventions** (page 43)

Unit 09: Technical drawing

OBJECTIVES
- Introduce architectural drawing methods
- Introduce and further technical drawing skills
- Introduce use of scale and proportion

Technical drawing can seem quite complicated at first, but once you understand the main principles of drafting you will become more accustomed to the skills needed to produce accurate technical drawings. The following stages illustrate the sequence of drafting the plan drawing.

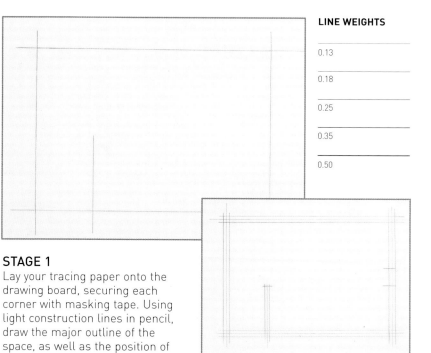

LINE WEIGHTS

0.13

0.18

0.25

0.35

0.50

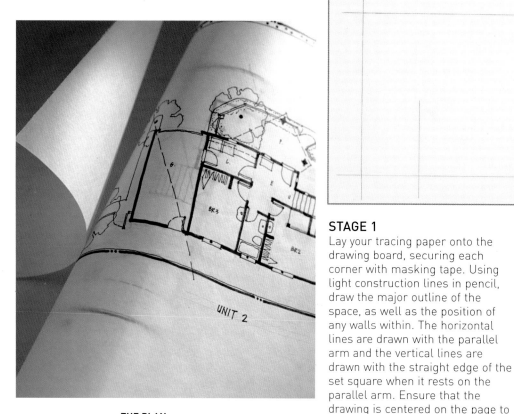

THE PLAN
A finished plan gives an accurate representation of the area measurements and layout of a space.

STAGE 1
Lay your tracing paper onto the drawing board, securing each corner with masking tape. Using light construction lines in pencil, draw the major outline of the space, as well as the position of any walls within. The horizontal lines are drawn with the parallel arm and the vertical lines are drawn with the straight edge of the set square when it rests on the parallel arm. Ensure that the drawing is centered on the page to allow for additional information, such as labels, titles, scale bars, and the key.

STAGE 2
Using a heavier line weight on top of the light construction line, show the position and thickness of major walls and structural elements such as columns and pillars.

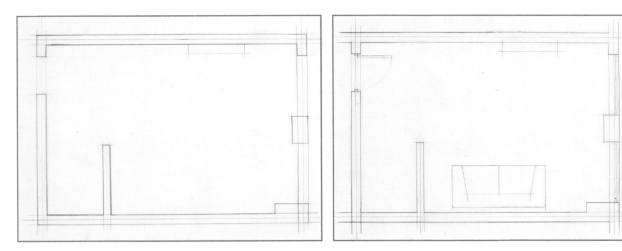

STAGE 3

Now carve out the major elements by showing the position of doorways, windows, fireplaces, and stairways. This line weight represents what is cut through.

STAGE 4

An intermediate line weight is then used to detail non-structural elements, including doors and stair treads as well as furniture. Your lightest line weight is used for fine detail, such as tiles, floorboards, glass, and door swings.

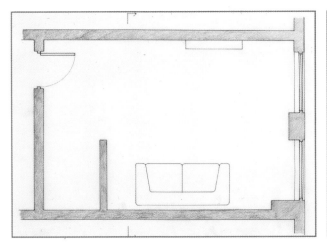

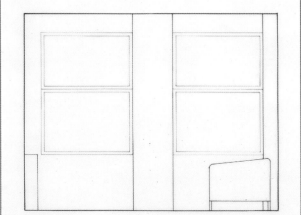

STAGE 5

Once you have completed the preparatory drawing in pencil, overlay it with a sheet of tracing paper and extract the final plan, using the correct line weights in ink. For graphic contrast, fill the walls in with a solid color so that anyone seeing your drawing will instantly visualize the space.

STAGE 6

Draft a section view, using the plan to project the information regarding widths and lengths. Referring to the survey notes, now add the vertical measurements to complete the drawing. The principle of line weights is the same for the vertical section as for the horizontal section.

See also

Unit 03: **Making a sketch model** (page 20)
Unit 07: **Architectural drawing conventions** (page 40)

Unit 10: Making presentation models

OBJECTIVES
- Introduce model-making techniques
- Understand important construction principles
- Learn to make a presentation model

Presentation models are an excellent way of communicating the final design scheme to a prospective client, both to explain and to seduce. Whatever your intended scheme, by using the simplest of tools and materials, you will learn to make a professional model that will showcase your design ideas. This unit covers the step-by-step process of making a presentation model, offering important construction principles as well as advice for achieving realistic textures and finishes.

Models are useful for all sorts of reasons. Sketch models allow designers to explore ideas, either with materials or forms, to generate more ideas, or simply to test planning possibilities. The presentation model is undoubtedly the most effective method of presenting a finished scheme to a client.

PREPARATION

CLEAR PRESENTATION
Models can be utilized and showcased as the central feature of the client presentation.

In order to make a presentation model, you will need two scale drawings—one plan and one section—to use as key dimensions when setting out the model. Your basic tools will be the same as those specified in Unit 03: Making a sketch model. These include a utility or matte knife with sharp blades (fine not heavy duty) as well as plastic cutting blades and a scalpel. You will also require an engineering square (4 in. or 100 mm) and a steel rule. The adhesives used to attach materials differ accordingly. When gluing edge-to-face joints, use polyvinyl acetate (PVA) of balsa cement. When gluing face-to-face joints, use non-repositionable spray adhesive, double-sided tape, or impact adhesive.

COLOR, TEXTURE, AND FINISH

A scale model represents a distant view of reality. Colors seen from afar are bluer and paler than they appear when seen up close. This is known as aerial perspective. When making a model, always consider using paler colors on the model than the actual colors. Avoid using paint or applying color directly by choosing self-colored materials. A wide range of papers and card is available in various colors, textures, and finishes, providing excellent substitutes for the materials you intend to use. Alternatively, you can make your own colored papers, using washes of watercolor paint.

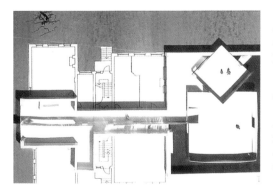

For wall surfaces, smooth paper or foam board represent smooth plaster very well, as do smooth colored papers. Rough plaster can be represented by using watercolor paper, which is available in many textures. A brick effect can be produced by drawing white or cream horizontal lines at intervals of 3 in. (75 mm) to scale on paper that is a softer version of the actual brick color. Tiling can be indicated by indenting lines in a regular grid into card, using a blunt point, a dead ball-point pen, or the edge of a palette knife.

For colored tiles, use a colored pencil lightly to render the surface of the white card, transforming the grid into white grout. Concrete or stone effects can be easily produced by washing balsa wood with white or pale-colored gouache—remember to paint the back with water, otherwise the wood will curl up. Wood effects are difficult to mimic at scale, however balsa wood and birch both have fine enough grain to stand in for other woods. To deepen wood colors, use watercolor in thin washes, but not wood stains as the absorption is too powerful and stains tend to bleed to other parts of the model.

FLOOR

The model should be built on a flat rigid base. Medium-density fiberboard (MDF) is the most stable material generally available. Unlike card, foam board, or plywood, it stays flat and does not warp. For a model that is 12 in. (300 mm) square, a ¼-in. (6-mm) MDF base works well; similarly, ½ in. (12 mm) is appropriate for a 24-in. (600-mm) square model. Before you construct the rest of the model, you will need to cover this base plate with a material that best represents the intended floor finish. The selected paper should be cut slightly oversized for the baseboard. Both the baseboard and the paper should then be covered with an even coat of spray adhesive. Lay one edge of the paper on the edge of the baseboard with the left hand, and the other edge up with the right hand. Gently stroke across the sheet with the left hand until the whole sheet is firmly fixed, ensuring that there are no air bubbles. Now turn the work upside down, trimming off the excess edges with a sharp scalpel. For a wooden floor finish you may lay a veneer (a very thin sheet of wood) directly onto the baseboard, using a strong glue such as an impact adhesive to fix it in place. The adhesive is applied to both surfaces and allowed to partially dry. The two sheets are then brought together under pressure. These glues are very strong for face-to-face joints. They produce petroleum vapor fumes, so should be used with care in a well-ventilated space.

PLAN

Either prick the plan drawing onto the base with a sharp scalpel, marking directly from the drawing itself, or carefully transfer the measurements with a ruler, marking faint marks or dots. Avoid drawing the lines directly onto the board, as these will show with slight discrepancies in the model.

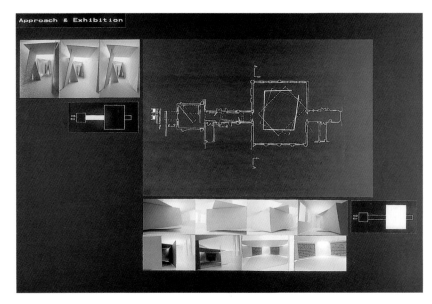

MAXIMIZING DIMENSIONS
Flat presentations should include model images to bring two-dimensional drawings to life.

MODEL FLOORING
Cover the base plate with the material representing the floor finish.

FIXING THE FINISH
Spray with adhesive, lay down one edge of the paper and stroke it down to remove air bubbles.

WALLS

Always use simple materials that are easy to cut, fix, and join. Card, foam board, balsa wood, and acrylic sheet are all materials that fulfil this criteria. Avoid using metal, hardwoods, plaster, or stone, as these are too difficult to handle and look incongruous at model scale. Represent these materials with paper effects, either with colored or textured papers. Prepare your wall material by covering card or foam board with a suitably colored or textured paper, using a spray adhesive. When measuring the walls, cut out strips of wall material to the same height, and then cut them to length, using an engineering square. This is a better method than measuring up each wall individually, as it ensures accuracy for both dimensions and angles.

JOINTS

When joining walls together, use a concealed butt joint. This is achieved easily with foam board. Having cut the wall to its longest dimension, move the engineering square back by the thickness of a sheet of foam board. Hold the scalpel with your index finger on the side of the blade to control the depth of the cut. Carefully cut through the upper skin of the paper and the polystyrene foam, without puncturing the lower skin of the paper. With the edge of a spare piece of foam board the surplus paper and foam can now be broken away with the scalpel. Using the edge of a spare piece of foam board, rub away the remnants of foam stuck to the lower skin of paper.

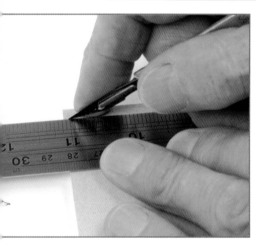

1. PREPARING THE MATERIAL
First prepare your material by covering it with suitably colored or textured paper.

2. CUTTING THE JOINT
Carefully cut through the upper skin of the paper and the foam, with your index finger on the side of the blade to control the depth of the cut.

3. MAKING A RABBET
Remove a strip of card or foam board to make a rabbet for a concealed butt joint.

4 and 5. GLUEING
Apply a minimal amount of glue and remove any excess.

CONSTRUCTION

Now you are ready to build the model up from the base. It is always best to build the model wall by wall onto the baseboard, rather than fitting all walls together and then onto the base. Erect the first wall using PVA glue. Make sure that the wall is vertical by using an engineering square to hold it in place while the glue is setting. The next wall should fit into position at a right angle. Applying a minimal amount of glue to this wall, stick it to the first wall and to the floor, using an engineering square to support it while the glue sets. Repeat this process until all the walls are firmly erected.

CURVED WALLS

Using card or foam board, walls can be curved by cutting through the skin on the outer side of the curve. Holding the scalpel with your index finger on the side of the blade, cut a series of equally spaced parallel slices. Be careful not to puncture the skin of the paper on the other side. Gently run the scalpel along each slice to make sure that each cut is equally deep. The foam board or card will now easily bend, opening up the slices. These can be covered with paper, using a good adhesive spray to fix the curve.

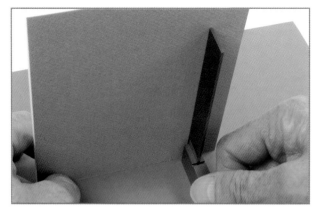

6. BUILDING THE MODEL
Build the model directly on the baseboard, and use an engineering square to hold the walls in place while the glue is setting.

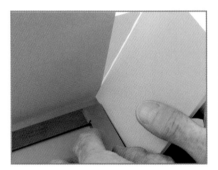

7. Fit the next wall in position.

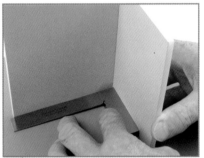

8. Make sure the walls are at right angles.

9. FITTING THE UPPER FLOOR
Work out the floor to ceiling height. Cut a strip of card accurately to this height, score vertically and fold.

10. This will provide an accurate prop to hold the floor in place.

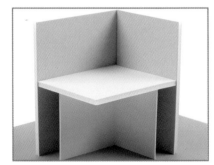

11. GLUEING IN PLACE
Use PVA to glue the floor in place. Remove the jig when the glue is set.

12. SLICING A CURVED WALL
Holding the scalpel with your index finger on the side of the blade, cut a series of equally spaced slices.

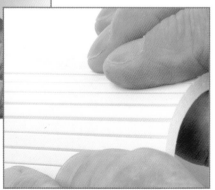

13. The foam board or card will now easily bend.

WINDOWS

To create a window, you will need to make a hole in the wall. Mark the dimension of the window lightly with a 5H pencil. Cut along one side from one corner almost to the other, without completing the cut. Do the same on each side of the opening. This ensures that the scalpel does not over-run. Then reverse the process, cutting from the uncut corners until the window opening is complete. To fit a piece of glazing into a piece of card or foam board, the hole and the glazing must be exactly the same size. The best method of glazing a window in a model is to make a sandwich construction. First cut the window material, either from acetate or 1 mm-thick acrylic to the size of the whole wall. Then cut the inner wall of paper, card, or foam board with the window hole. Next, cut the outer wall with the window hole. Finish by assembling the whole sandwich using double-sided tape as your adhesive.

STAIRCASES

Once you have designed your stair (see Unit 07: Architectural drawing conventions) make a simple and accurate jig consisting of a pair of strings. Separate these with pieces of card. This can form the structure for a simple staircase, act as a temporary support for a cantilever stair while the glue is setting, or be reduced to the central spine. This simple method can be adapted to make almost any type of staircase.

14. MAKING A WINDOW
Make the inner wall and the outer wall. Cut the acetate or acrylic to the same size as the whole wall.

15. ASSEMBLING THE WINDOW
Apply double-sided adhesive tape.

16. Fit one piece of the wall to the acetate or acrylic.

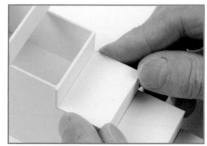

17. The completed window.

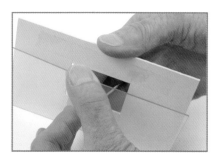

18. STAIRCASES
Make an accurate jig consisting of a pair of strings.

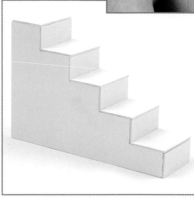

19. First fit all the risers.

20. Then the treads.

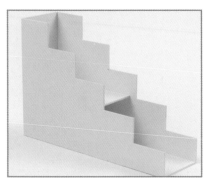

21. The completed staircase.

22. For a cantilever staircase, use the jig to hold the steps in place while the glue is setting.

SPIRAL STAIRCASES

A spiral staircase with a central newel can be made very easily using the following method. Draw the stair plan on card. Cut the circles, but leave the newel hole. Make a jig of card to hold the newel horizontal. Mark up the newel with risers. Cut a bird mouth to allow for the newel hole. Stick the steps carefully onto the balancing newel. Use balsa cement as it sets quickly. As each step sets, turn the newel and proceed.

23. SPIRAL STAIRCASES Cut a bird mouth to allow for the newel.

24. Hold the newel horizontally on the jig with double-sided tape, and stick the steps carefully onto the newel.

25. As each step sets, turn the newel and proceed.

THREE-DIMENSIONAL CURVES

Spheres and three-dimensional elements are difficult to make, so it is best to search for ready-made shapes. There are specialist suppliers for the model-making industry, and some professional workshops will make pieces to order for a fee. Alternatively, create your own piece by making a solid core of plaster the shape of the piece, painting it with a release agent (such as soap), and covering with layers of tissue paper soaked in glue. You can also use glass fiber-reinforced resin.

TREES, ROCKS, AND WATER

Trees can be spun from wire. Cork bark can be obtained from florists to make very convincing cliffs and rocks. Any shiny surface—for example, glossy paper, varnish, or acrylic sheet—can represent water. The darker the material, the better the reflection. Remember that water seldom looks blue unless it is a very sunny day.

PHOTOGRAPHING MODELS

Always take photographs of your models; these provide an excellent opportunity to illustrate presentation drawings and are good material for your archives when the model ages or gets damaged. Remember that the most realistic views are the ones that recreate the standing eye level. Take photos that give and promote human scale by bringing the eye level down to the correct scale within the model. Experiment with the use of natural and artificial light for daytime and night shots of the space. Using different lenses, manipulate wide-angle views, and alter the compositions slightly within each frame, to help inspire creative photographs. For high-contrast images, use black and white film and carefully controlled lighting. For realistic shots, use color with natural lighting.

See also
Unit 05: **Drawing material** (page 34)
Unit 06: **Human dimensions** (page 36)
Unit 07: **Architectural drawing conventions** (page 40)

Unit 11: Axonometric and perspective drawing

OBJECTIVES
- Understand how to construct 3D drawings
- Understand how to use drawing conventions
- Learn to construct a technical drawing

Three-dimensional drawings are, by their very nature, realistic representations of space, so they allow us to model space as effectively as possible on paper, helping us to understand the spatial qualities of a given site. This unit explores the step-by-step construction of three-dimensional drawings as a useful tool to further the understanding of spatial design.

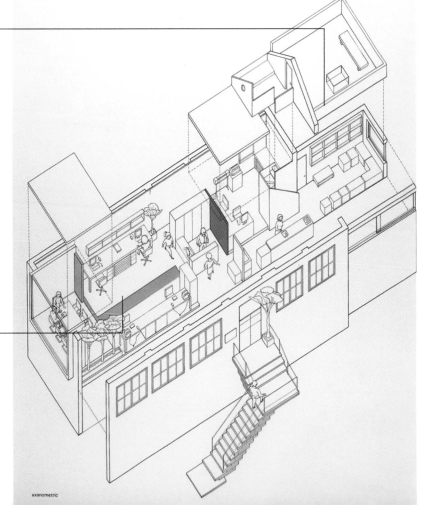

axonometric

Elements are exploded, using a dotted line to represent the movement and the position of detachment—upward, downward, or sideways along the given axis.

A COMPLETE PRESENTATION
This exploded axonometric of a retail space is presented together with design references, images, and two-dimensional drawings to reinforce the design concept to the client.

Axonometric drawings can be enhanced by rendering. Colored elements illustrate different material relationships and describe the zoning of interior spaces.

AXONOMETRICS
The axonometric drawing is particularly useful because it allows the plan, section, and elevation views to be represented in one drawing. The axonometric resembles a model view from above the space so that the whole scheme is viewed at once. Axonometrics are easily constructed using the true plan to project each point from the plan to a given height. The information concerning heights, widths, and lengths can all be taken from the finished section and plan views. Axonometrics can be constructed using varying degrees of plan orientation with an emphasis at 45/45 degrees, 60/30 degrees, or at complete 90-degree angles to the horizontal. With each orientation, the total always equals 90 degrees.

CONVEYING THE EFFECT
A well depicted axonometric can communicate and project the spatial qualities of a scheme, showing the overall layout of an interior as well as describing the use of materials and the ambient feel of interior lighting effects.

STAGE 1 Setting up the axonometric drawing

Following on from the plans in Unit 09, explode the axonometric. Place the plan on the drawing board, ensuring that the lines on either side of the drawing sit at 45 degrees to the parallel motion. Now place the drawing onto the board, using masking tape to fix each corner of the page securely to the board. Next, overlay a sheet of tracing paper on top, making sure that the page is centered over the drawing. You are now ready to draw your axonometric.

STAGE 2 Projecting heights

Begin constructing the axonometric drawing by drafting the three major axes in a clockwise direction. Trace the floor line and project the walls up to the ceiling height of the scale used. Use your set square to draw all vertical lines, ensuring that it sits squarely on the parallel motion for accuracy. Use your parallel motion to draw all horizontal lines. When drawing, remember to pull the line up or across; never push a line, as this can cause a less accurate result.

STAGE 3 Inking

Once you have drafted the axonometric drawing in pencil, you are ready to overlay and trace with ink. Drafting in ink is a real skill, and requires patience. Never rush your drawing when inking. Make sure you move from left to right and from top to bottom to avoid smudging and allow the ink to dry while you continue to draw. To define and detail the drawing effectively, you may use different line weights in the same way as with sections and plans (see Unit 07: Architectural drawing conventions).

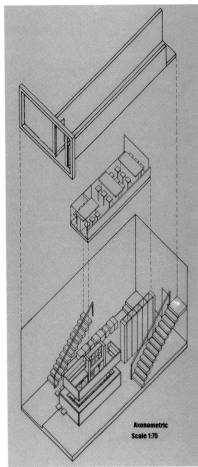

Axonometric
Scale 1:75

EXPLODED LEVELS
A bar design scheme is exploded into three significant parts to illustrate three different areas of activity within a double height space. The top floor separates arrival and the facade, the second space reveals a private lounging area, and the basement floor accommodates the main bar area.

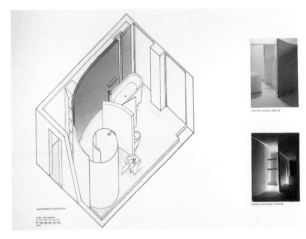

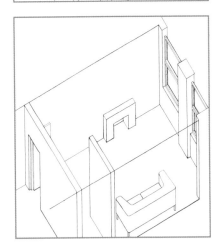

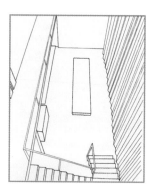

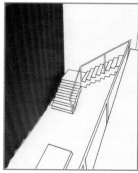

PERSPECTIVES
A series of perspectives gives different viewpoints within an interior to give a sense of double height space.

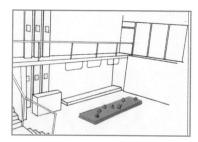

PERSPECTIVES

Perspectives provide the most realistic view in terms of three-dimensional drawing, because they locate us physically within the space, corresponding to what we would actually see. The perspective is based on our point of view, having an exact position within the space, and viewing the space at a certain eye level. The basic principles of perspective drawing are therefore based on the position of the viewer within the space, and a height of eye level.

STAGE 1 Setting up the perspective

Place the plan and the selected elevation on the drawing board. Leave enough space between the plan and the elevation to draw the perspective. Lay a new sheet of tracing paper over the plan and the elevation, and trace over the elevation. You are now ready to construct your perspective.

STAGE 2 The eye level

The eye level of a person standing is drawn at 5 feet (1.5 m), but the eye level can be drawn at any height, depending on what you want to see. In perspective, if you want to show more of the floor, a higher eye level is required. If you wish to show more of the ceiling, a seated eye level is more desirable.

STAGE 3 The position of the viewer

When drawing a space in perspective, you can illustrate the view from one side, from the middle, or from the opposite side of the space. This position, whichever you choose, is called the position of the viewer. Decide which view you wish to take and draw it on the plan, extending this line through to the elevation. The combination of the eye level with the line from the position of the viewer gives you the vanishing point (VP).

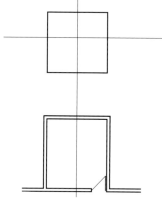

ELEVATION
Eye level is indicated at the desired height. The combination of the eye level and position of the viewer gives the vanishing point.

PLAN
The plan shows the position of the viewer, with a central line that extends up to the elevation to give the vanishing point

STAGE 4 The cone of vision

The cone of vision is how much the eye sees. It is therefore important to check that the position of the viewer is correct. A cone of 60 degrees is taken from the viewer. It is usually drawn as 30 degrees on both sides of the line from the position of the viewer on the plan. Everything that falls within this cone of vision can be drawn in perspective. Anything that falls outside the cone of vision will be distorted.

On a separate sheet of tracing paper, draw a perpendicular line. On both sides of this line, draw an angle of 30 degrees. Place this over the plan, along the line from the position of the viewer. You may extend this line outside the plan if you wish, but the cone of vision must include everything that you want to see in the perspective. When you have decided what you want to see in the perspective, mark the viewer on the plan. Using the vanishing point (VP), draw a line from the VP through each corner of the elevation, to form the ceiling, walls, and floor of your perspective. You are now ready to draw objects in perspective.

STAGE 5 Drawing the object

To draw an object, you will need information about its width, height, and depth. The width of the object can be taken from the plan to the base of the elevation. Connect these points on the base of the elevation with the VP, and bring them into the perspective. This is the width of the object in perspective. The height is then drawn to scale on the elevation in one of the following two ways. Using the reference points of the width of the object, project the height upward, connecting this height with the VP, and then bring it into the perspective. Alternatively, use the right-hand corner of the elevation as a height line. Measure the height of the object in scale along this line, and connect it with the VP. Bring it into the perspective along the side wall of the perspective. Whichever method is used, height and width are always connected with the vanishing point and brought into the perspective.

Depth is created in perspective by constructing a measuring line. On the plan, measure the distance between the viewer and the wall from which the elevation is taken. Take this measurement, and transfer it out from the side of the elevation. This becomes the measuring line. Connect the measuring line to the eye level to form the measuring point (MP).

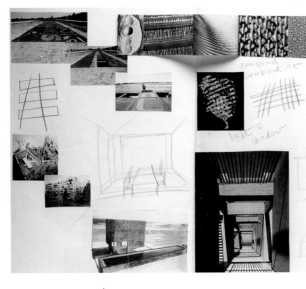

PHOTOS
Photographic perspectives are a good way of exploring the exact position of the vanishing point.

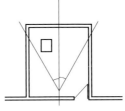

CONE OF VISION
30 degrees to either side of the position of the viewer gives the cone of vision. The cone demarcates what the perspective view will show.

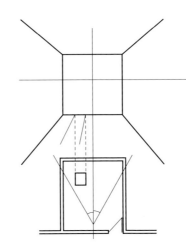

The width of the object is taken from the plan to the base of the elevation. Connecting these points with the vanishing point brings the lines into perspective.

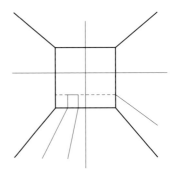

Height is drawn to scale either by using reference points given by the width or by using the elevation as a height line.

Now measure the distance between the object and the rear wall in scale. Transfer this measurement onto the measuring line, starting from the elevation; mark as B. Draw a construction line from MP through B, and bring it to the wall of the perspective. Once the construction line hits the wall, draw a straight line across from this point until it meets the width lines. You now have width and depth in perspective.

STAGE 6 Adding the height

To complete the perspective, draw in the height. If you have marked the height on the elevation using the width points, connect all four corners of the object in perspective, with the height lines in perspective.

If you have used the corner of the elevation as a height line, and brought the height along the side wall of the perspective, bring perpendicular lines up from the reference points on the side wall of the perspective until they hit the height line. At this point, take a straight line across the perspective. From the object in the perspective, draw lines up from all four corners until they hit the

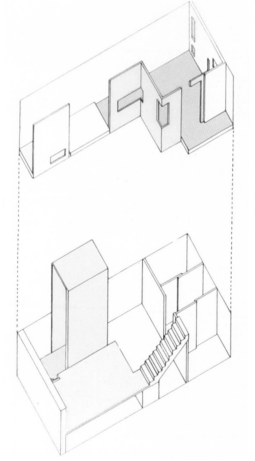

VISUAL AID
Axonometric drawings are essentially model-like in character, allowing us an unnatural view from above the space. When presented together with two-dimensional drawings, axonometrics become important visual aids, describing the material properties of the line drawings.

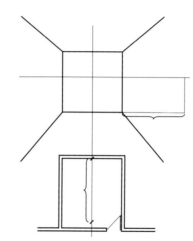

DISTANCE
The distance between the object and rear wall is transferred to the measuring line.

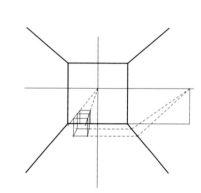

HEIGHT, WIDTH, DEPTH
The vanishing point is used to connect the height, and the measuring point gives the width and depth.

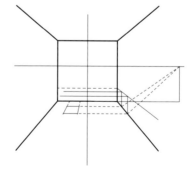

CONSTRUCTION LINE
A construction line from the measuring point into the perspective gives the width and depth.

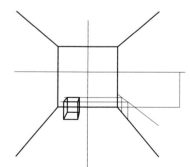

FINISHED PERSPECTIVE
To complete the perspective, connect all four corners of the object with the height in perspective.

height lines. Connect all four corners at this height. You should now have the object in perspective. Any object can be drawn in perspective following these rules.

General principles apply when constructing all perspectives, whether it is a quick sketch or an accurate measured drawing. Any object or space can be tackled using the following rules.

CONE OF VISION
The cone of vision shows how much the eye sees before things appear distorted. Here the cone illustrates what is seen from the standing position.

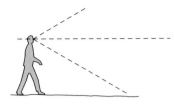

STANDING EYE LEVEL
When standing, eye level remains consistent within perspectives whether people are in the foreground or background of a drawing. The eyes are on the same level as though they are hung on a washing line.

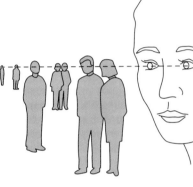

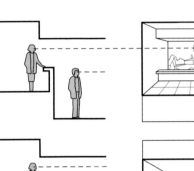

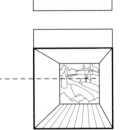

DIFFERENT LEVELS
Standard eye height is contrasted with a high eye level in this drawing to give different views of the same space. From the high eye level, the upper part of the space is seen. At the standard eye level more of the floor is seen.

SEATED EYE LEVEL
In a seated position the eye level is lower so that more of the ceiling is seen. When the eye level and the position of the viewer are combined, this determines the vanishing point in perspective. All objects diminish towards infinity.

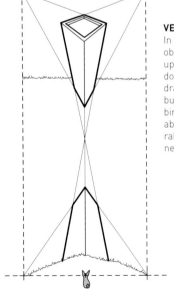

VERTICAL VIEWS
In perspective, objects can diminish upward or downward. This drawing illustrates a building seen from a bird's eye view (from above) and from a rabbit's view (from near the ground).

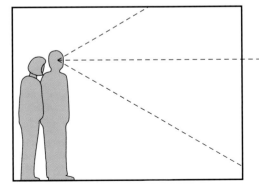

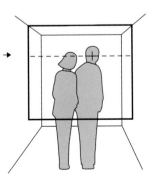

LINE OF SIGHT
The line of sight leads to the vanishing point as the cone opens.

Unit 12: Computer-aided design

OBJECTIVES
- Introduce the basic principles of CAD
- Understand the context within which CAD is used
- Understand the use of CAD within the design process

DESIGN PRESENTATION
This image from a house extension design incorporates a digital picture of the proposed garden seen through the sliding doors.

Computer-aided design (CAD) systems are used for constructing architectural drawings, as well as developing ideas within a design process. The scope and purposes of CAD are important not just for drafting ideas, but also for developing and modeling them. Although there are different CAD software systems, this unit will cover the basic principles and ideas applicable to any CAD system. We will explore the importance of the computer as a tool to further enhance and help you to enjoy the activity of design.

The innovation of technology has moved CAD software from being merely a drafting tool to a technology capable of communicating design expressions in the early stages of design ideas. CAD technology is able to reflect and support design thinking, model design strategies, and provide a deeper awareness of architectural space. It does so by providing the designer with possibilities, expanding the individual's ability to test form, shape, and view by bringing the design closer to its built reality.

Designers employ CAD systems for a number of reasons. CAD is able to create, manipulate, analyze, and represent design possibilities. Computers can carry out rapid and complex calculations, process information and data, and help to analyze design in terms of economic, functional, and environmental requirements. Drawing on a computer saves time and allows quick access to revise design changes when necessary. Moreover, the computer allows the designer to employ a different set of skills more closely linked to the process of simulation, generating a greater degree of realism. Walk-throughs and movement simulations allow designers to experience and visualize the significance of their designs, as well as communicate these qualities to others.

INFORMATION PACKAGE
CAD drawings enable designers to draw, dimension, and layer information quickly to create a package of drawings.

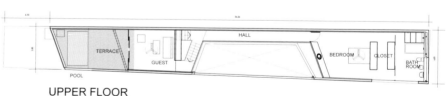

UPPER FLOOR

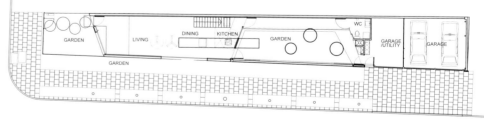

CAD OBJECTS

CAD objects fall into two different categories. The first group consists of two-dimensional objects, suitable for plan or section drawings. Line is the most basic 2D object in the CAD system, with straight lines being the most frequently used 2D objects. Line also has the most attributes and lines can be varied in thickness, color, and style, and given specific end points, such as arrowheads. Because different lines can represent different layers within a drawing, styles and colors become part of a system denoting services or structural elements. These 2D drawing symbols are used to represent fixtures, fittings, structural, and non-structural objects, such as furniture. Other elements include arcs, circles, polygons, planar shapes, and grids.

The second group consists of three-dimensional objects, which are modeled and extruded up from two-dimensional (horizontal) objects to become planes, such as wall, floor, or roof (vertical) elements. As well as rectangular extrusions, CAD offers a range of predefined 3D volumes once length, width, height, and radius data is given. Alternatively, shapes can be drawn directly, without giving data, by using the mouse to stretch objects to the required dimensions. Perspective and axonometric drawings are displayed as "wire frame" shapes and lines, to define the surface, shape, and volume of spaces. These three-dimensional drawings can be rotated in CAD to provide different views within the space.

WHICH PROGRAM IS RIGHT FOR YOU?

Computer-aided design software programs change and develop quite quickly as manufacturers introduce new features and new programs. Overall they can be divided into two areas: those for professional interior design and architectural use, and those meant for home and possibly small business use.

Professional programs include Autocad (by far the most widely used program for construction and design), Microstation (architectural) and Vectorworks for design and technical use. All of these and other similar ones are expensive to buy and require training and time to understand and make the fullest use of them.

For most straightforward use, particularly to plan and design small-scale domestic design including room layouts, a professional system is unnecessary and over-complicated. A search of the Internet under CAD for interior design will identify a number of quite simple, inexpensive programs such as SmartDraw or 3Dspacer, which enable the user with little practice to construct layouts that begin to utilize the capabilities of digital design. The software incorporates preloaded examples of rooms, furniture, and fittings, which can be selected and manipulated to fit new dimensions and specifications.

Initial research will pay dividends. Look at manufacturers' websites on the Internet, get a feeling for what different programs can do relative to their cost, and relate that to what you want to achieve.

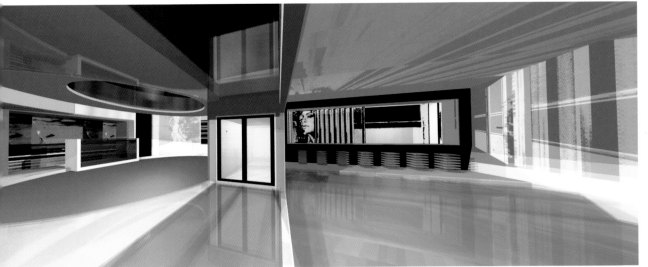

FINAL DESIGN
This digital image gives a panoramic view around an interior space and represents the modern essence of the design.

CASE STUDY 03: Flexible space

THE BRIEF
To remodel an existing living space by opening up the interior so that function and practicality create light and spacious living.
Budget: Small. The designer is the client, working from home.
Design: Brook Fieldhouse Associates

What is meant by good design? Well-planned and considered design can provide improved and effective environments that fit the needs of the user. The importance of good design is tested both by our day-to-day routine and by the practicalities and necessities of light and space. In the following case study, the design is realized by slight modifications to an existing plan. It highlights the clever use of space as a fluid and flexible raw material.

MINIMALIST DESIGN

This two-bedroom apartment within a riverside development proclaims the importance of minimalist living, with over 15 percent of its total volume being built-in storage, and 75 percent of that figure being closed away. The aim of the design is primarily to create as much flexible space as possible by maximizing storage while retaining the apartment's two-bedroom status. With the designer working from home, the need for a studio-office became the key factor in reorganizing the interior spaces.

LIVING SPACE
Modern furniture has been chosen to complement the architectural style of the apartment. A design vocabulary of clean lines and simple details avoids visual clutter.

THE PLAN
The main design intervention in the planning of this scheme allows two spaces that were originally separate to become connected, facilitating maximum usage. Here, the plan clearly indicates how intended activities are carried out, by locating positions of furniture, fixtures, and fittings.

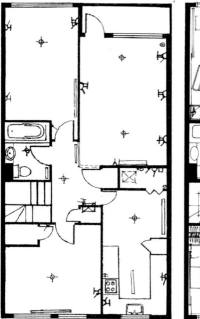

Folding glass panels allow the user to enjoy light and view, doubling the living space and connecting the interior to the exterior.

A dotted rectangle indicates the position of the bed once it has been folded out of the wall system, changing the office into a second bedroom.

Furniture is placed aesthetically and practically within the space, responding to interior and exterior views for maximum relaxation.

The sliding partition represents the threshold between two spaces, allowing activities to change from work in the daytime to rest at night.

OPEN SPACE
Patio doors are replaced by sliding and folding glass panels, opening up the interior to views of the river.

DESIGN FEATURES

It is important to recognize that often the most dramatic changes to a space do not have to be structural. In this case, a non-structural stud partition wall is removed between the second bedroom and the sitting area and replaced with three sliding panels. This creates a space 20 feet (6 meters) wide, which forms an L-shaped floor plan. The open-plan space is now able to accommodate a studio, a foldaway bed, and a dining alcove. Depending on the intended activity and the time of day, the spaces can be opened up or closed off for privacy.

OFFICE SPACE
A neutral color scheme allows objects to appear more prominently displayed, giving a clear indication of the intended activities in each area.

STORAGE SPACE
Storage and shelving is maximized to keep surfaces and floors free. Exposed bookshelves house materials in constant use, while objects that are used less frequently (which might cause clutter) are stored out of sight.

DESIGN DETAILS

To further enhance the feeling of light and space, wall panels are backlit and remain raised off the floor to emphasize the floor space. Hidden storage keeps the interior uncluttered and creates a low-dust environment. All central ceiling light fixtures are removed and replaced with ambient wall lights and freestanding lamps. Walls and floors are kept white to maximize the interior space. This allows the placing of interior furniture to appear more prominent and clearly defines the areas of proposed activity.

VERSATILE SPACE
Minimalist office space creates maximum flexibility and offers a blank canvas for different living/working activities.

MULTIFUNCTIONAL SPACE
At night, the space is transformed into a second bedroom.

Sliding panels conceal office storage and reveal a fold-down bed.

RECEPTION SPACE
When entertaining, office and bed areas can be concealed to make way for open-plan dining.

Furniture is used for all activities, whether work, life, or play.

CASE STUDY 04: Updating the dated

THE BRIEF
To update a bathroom by redesigning and enlarging the interior to create a practical space that is a haven of aesthetic luxury.
Budget: Small. The client is a young professional looking for the "wow factor."
Designers: Forster, Inc.

From time to time, an interior space can lose its true purpose, becoming less efficient and less sympathetic to lifestyle requirements. In the following case study a tired and dated bathroom is redesigned and brought back to life and in the process it creates a new "wow factor" for the home. Exciting design features and cutting-edge materials come together to create and transform a practical bathroom into a haven of luxury and light.

PENTHOUSE BATHROOM
All too often, practical spaces are approached with a lack of imagination and aesthetic inventiveness. This penthouse bathroom illustrates that a functional space can be entirely practical while forming a dramatic focal point within the home. The existing bathroom was too small, so the designers decided to extend the space into a large hallway. The creation of a curved wall enabled them to make efficient use of the space and doubled as an exciting design feature for the entrance to the apartment. Despite a small budget, the design team was able to create a complete transformation for the whole residence.

INDIVIDUALITY
Creating a special design feature shows innovation and individuality as well as being a highly practical design solution tailored for the user. The curved wall is made from a curved stainless steel frame, which supports a double skin of transparent acrylic.

MATERIALS AND FINISHES

Using state-of-the-art materials and clever lighting effects enabled the designers to test their ideas with new technologies while working with a team of specialized engineers. The curved wall was constructed from a laser-cut stainless steel frame, with a double layer of translucent polypropylene. Made in several pieces, the wall was delivered via the elevator and assembled on site. Colored film panels provide a contrast to the mosaic floor, while the wall is lit by a dimmable neon bulb at the base. A stainless steel cover is a clever detail used to conceal the bath pipes. The final effect achieves a new concept for the "bathroom" by replacing it with a translucent skin that glows day and night.

As the client remarks: "When you're lying in the bath, you feel like you're surrounded by a halo. The light radiates through the oranges and the reds of the acrylic wall and the whole bathroom simply glows."

METALLIC DETAILS
Smooth and shiny accents of metal are present in fixtures and fittings. A stainless steel detail provides a neat finish to conceal bath pipes.

COLOR INTERACTION
Cool blue walls and a pale blue mosaic floor set off the warm curve of the wall, creating subtle color contrasts and harmonies.

FLOATING COLOR
Orange and yellow fields of color float within the acrylic wall to create an ambient and luxurious effect from within the bathing space.

3 Design projects

This chapter provides an in-depth look at a range of stages within a design project, bringing together all aspects of the design process covered so far, from concept to presentation and completion.

Many different skills are needed for the work stages of a project: assessing client requirements, undertaking site analysis, writing a brief, and scheduling an existing site, as well as space planning and designing. Design case studies in this chapter provide important examples of the nature and breadth of interior design, while illustrating the importance of conceiving the project as a package.

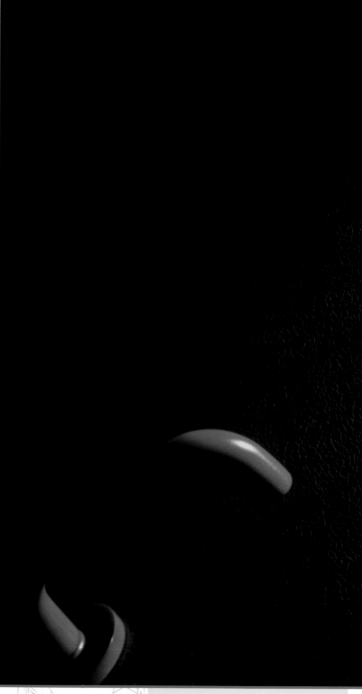

Unit 13 | Creating a brief
(page 70)

13

Unit 14 | Writing a client profile
(page 72)

14

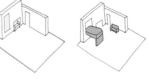

See also
Unit 01: **Site research and building study** (page 12)
Unit 04: **Developing an idea** (page 24)

Unit 13: Creating a brief

OBJECTIVES
- Learn to devise a working brief
- Build a client profile
- Work to client requirements

Working to a brief means that you are working for others and responding to criteria that you have not chosen. The brief shapes the design process, generates the final design, and helps simplify and organize the project into stages. There is more than one decision to be made, and a design process is never a straight line. This unit will cover the processes of creating a brief, devising a clear description of what needs to be done by defining the task.

USING COLORED PERSPECTIVES
A brief for a commercial interior is proposed using quick concept sketches that use corporate colors reflecting the client company's identity.

The start of a brief is often the most creative point of a project, where most of the questions need to be asked and where relationships between key individuals are set. It is the designer's responsibility to analyze, evaluate, and interpret complex pieces of information into the form of a design brief. This is an essential tool that defines the parameters of the project by prioritizing its aims and objectives. A designer may often consider several possibilities before deciding on a final idea or outcome. Having clear design criteria can help when testing various options.

THE DESIGN PROCESS

A design project has a lifetime, determined by the duration of the process from concept through to completion. When creating a brief, the designer will go through a series of design stages. The first stage involves evaluating what exists through site analysis, research, and compiling relevant data. This stage identifies the givens, or the restrictions. These are things that the designer has inherited and has no ability to change. This may include the location of the site or the size of the spaces.

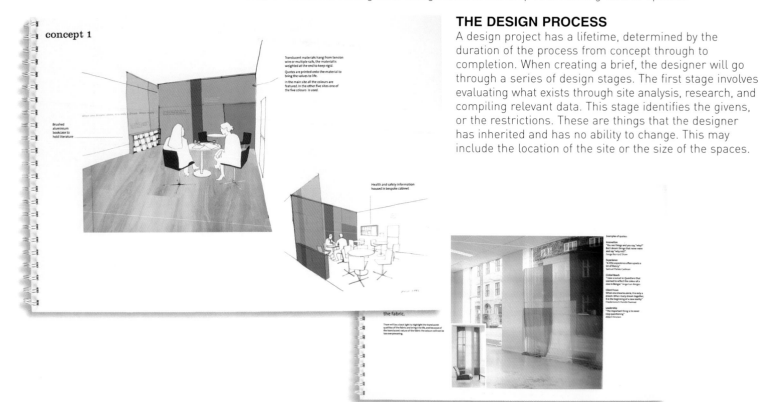

The second stage involves analyzing what is required by focusing on the client's needs and by planning the steps needed to fulfill the brief. This stage includes considering the practical as well as the impractical wishes of the client. The designer has to interpret these requirements in light of the problems or solutions offered by the former stage, in this way tightening up the brief.

The third stage is a synthesis of the previous stages. The designer considers what is possible when integrating the practical and conceptual aims of the brief. The designer includes all restrictions to determine the outcome of the brief. These could be physical, financial, or legal restraints, all of which will have to be taken into account before the proposal is reached.

CONCEPT BOARDS

In the initial stages of a project, concept presentations can help a client visualize the spirit of the idea by suggesting how the idea could become a potential scheme. Concept boards can either be general or specific, depending on the client and the project. They help to define the brief by setting the design idea into a framework of choices and possibilities (see Unit 04, Developing an idea).

CREATIVE INPUTS

The project should encourage divergent thinking from the outset. The designer should be open to initial responses and be prepared to move away from these to test other ideas. A creative investment at the beginning often generates interesting ideas at the end.

DESIGN CRITERIA

Sometimes the designer will be aware of the qualities that need to be achieved. This means being able to judge what is good or bad about the design, whether the aim is practical or functional, aesthetic, user-friendly or ecologically sound. Design criteria are defined by the brief and should be reviewed regularly to ensure that the design task has been achieved.

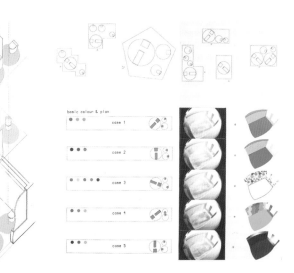

BRIEF POSSIBILITIES
A series of design options are created with a flexible bathing space.

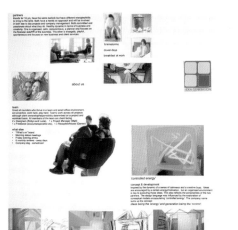

DISPLAYING A COMMERCIAL PROFILE
A concept board breaks down the company profile to investigate the site, its location, the company identity, and its staff hierarchy.

THE PROJECT

Choose a site and create a brief for an imaginary project. Use a space or a series of spaces that you are familiar with, either at work, at home or in a public space that you would consider improving. Begin by deciding on the scale of the project and then define the brief by listing all the necessary requirements for the proposed design task.

The process

Your brief should include information about the existing site, providing important restrictions to give the parameters of the design task. Now consider what should be proposed by developing your brief against the following questions. Who is your client? What do they want to improve? Is it possible? If so, how? Write your brief on one side of a single sheet of paper. You are now ready to write a client profile.

See also
Unit 04: **Developing an idea** (page 24)

Unit 14: Writing a client profile

OBJECTIVES
- Learn to understand your client
- Build a client profile
- Work to client requirements

Understanding your client means a lot more than simply responding to user requirements. The client may bring with them their own ideas and aspirations, but remember that your client is a layperson—a non-designer who cannot make the design happen without you. It is the designer's job to interpret and give the client what they want, which may not be the same as what they ask for. Learn to discern the essentials about your client by creating a profile that identifies and targets their needs, interests, and lifestyle.

CONSIDERATE DESIGN
A designer should always consider the
workforce when designing an office space.

The client has the responsibility of directing the designer at the start, but as the initial excitement fades, clients can become conservative and guarded against new ideas. Often the client needs to be persuaded and reassured that new ideas produce new possibilities for the design. Be sensitive to the needs of the client, as this relationship is pivotal to the whole process. Keep the lines of communication open. It is a good idea to predetermine the work stages and review these together with the client. This allows the designer to avoid progressing in the wrong direction, which can be costly and time-consuming. Thorough research can help you to plan and identify the main areas of focus for the client.

Begin by writing a client profile. List your client's requirements and prioritize them with a time schedule of what needs to be done and when it will be completed. Make sure you keep a diary of all your meetings so that any changes or adjustments are recorded. Get the client on board so that they feel confident and included in the process. Prepare them for

Access

Entrance

Library

Section CC

Section DD

Meeting Room

home:

where my memories reside

which I leave for the pleasure of returning again and again

CLIENT PROFILE

CLIENT REQUIREMENTS
The concept board above illustrates the user requirements of a gallery space and considers disability access. The board at left maps personal memories of a client.

THE PROJECT
Invent an imaginary client or, better still, use a friend to create a client profile. Imagine that you are designing a residential space for your client. Plan a checklist of questions you want to ask and be prepared to consider ideas that are different from your own.

The process
Having created a realistic client, you need to explore what they will require. Begin by creating a client profile. Identify any important information that would be relevant and list age, gender, occupation, economic status, and any information about lifestyle, interests, and hobbies. Most important requirements are generally determined by lifestyle values. If your client is young, single, and has a professional career, their lifestyle requirements will be different from those of someone with a small family. Draw some conclusions from your client profile; these will give you the beginnings of a brief for planning your design in Unit 16.

what is to come, as change can be difficult. When things need revising, agree to any changes with a signature. This will cover any disagreements and disputes that may arise and will allow both client and designer to know where they stand. Give your client an opportunity to describe any imagined ideas for the space—it could be helpful to show a series of interior ideas in the form of images and discover which kinds of ideas are favored and why. Get the client to prioritize what is most important, as well as what is of least importance.

Redesign of commercial space for a creative design office.

1) Is the company being rebranded? Consider how to use the company logo to inform design.

2) Analyze the staff hierachy and user requirements.

3) Interview the staff about work patterns—what works? What would they like to change?

4) Prioritize design work stages—source furniture, lighting, decorators, etc.

5) Prepare a presentation to the staff before work begins.

Example checklist for a commercial client.

See also

Unit 13: **Creating a brief** (page 70)

Unit 15: Writing a design proposal

OBJECTIVES
- Learn to formulate your ideas
- Write a design proposal
- Apply your understanding of design criteria

The design proposal is the mission statement that drives the design scheme. It enables the designer to formulate ideas into a strategy, to tackle and solve design problems, and to explain what they wish to achieve in the project by defining how it will maximize the qualities of an interior space. In this unit, you will be introduced to the methods of writing a design proposal, as well as reflecting on the methods and skills involved in the process.

MANAGING EXPECTATIONS
Even though the proposal marks the start of the project, the client will be expecting the final product—so make sure your presentation is to a high standard.

A proposal is a piece of purposeful writing. It defines the aims and objectives of a design scheme by setting down the parameters of the task. This is determined largely by the initial brief, as well as by the client's requirements. The proposal should illustrate what you, the designer, intend to do, given your set of design criteria.

Before you begin writing your proposal, make a checklist of all the existing elements that you have to work with. Make sure you include everything that you have inherited from the site, even though you may intend to change these. Next, list the things you want to remove, and then the things you wish to introduce. These checklists allow you to compare the existing with what you intend to propose. Now evaluate the client's priorities and requirements once more. Does your design respond to the criteria with which you are working? If so, you are now ready to write your proposal, outlining your strategy for the space.

When beginning your proposal, introduce the project by explaining what, where, when, why, and how the interior will encompass change. It is often a good idea to set out your proposal under a series of headings. Start off by providing the existing site location and its description. You can include important factors from your site research that may prove central considerations of the design, as well as any building or structural analysis. You should follow up by providing the brief (given by the client) and the brief analysis (interpreted by the designer). This determines your design criteria, and shows that you have considered the major factors that govern the overall design strategy. Once these initial headings have been established, identify the concept by explaining how it will translate into a design in stages. These stages should include initial responses to the brief and sketch design ideas, as well as design development. Diagrams, sketches, and drawings should accompany the design proposal (where possible and relevant) to show how the final scheme will be achieved. Remember that a strong design proposal is visual as well as factual.

The brief (from the client) and the brief analysis (from the designer) determine your design criteria.

PROJECT

Now turn to Unit 16: Planning your design. Using your "client profile" from Unit 14, summarize your design proposal on a sheet of paper. Make sure you include as much information as possible by following the prompts below.

Process checklist

STAGE 1 Identify the existing and proposed elements for the design.

STAGE 2 Revise the design brief and prioritize the client's requirements.

STAGE 3 Develop the design strategy in response to the design criteria.

STAGE 4 Identify the design concept.

STAGE 5 Illustrate the proposal.

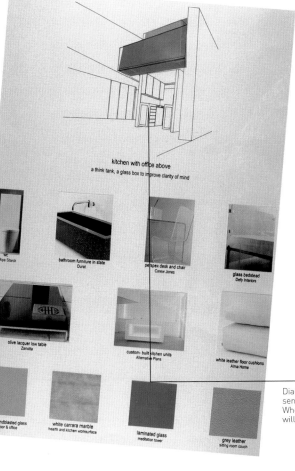

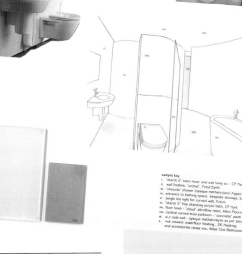

Diagrams, sketches, and drawings give a visual sense of how the final scheme will be achieved. Where possible indicate any design features that will affect the experience of the space.

KEEPING THE CLIENT ENGAGED

A strong idea or concept should be illustrated to help convince the client at the proposal stage.

See also

Unit 11: **Axonometric and perspective drawing** (page 54)
Unit 14: **Writing a client profile** (page 72)
Unit 15: **Writing a design proposal** (page 74)
Unit 18: **Building materials** (page 90)
Unit 25: **Creating a sample board** (page 112)

Unit 16: Planning your design

OBJECTIVES
- Learn to plan an interior space
- Work to a set brief
- Produce a presentation of your design

Planning your ideas with a view to creating a design scheme is perhaps the most rewarding task that a designer has to undertake. This is where your creative input is most effective, and where your ideas culminate to become a powerful reality. This unit will allow you to bring together all the design know-how developed in the previous units, and help you apply and realize your own design skills in the form of a set project.

Bubble diagrams transform conceptual ideas into planning possibilities. They help to depict the positions of spatial activities and their circulation.

CONCEPTUAL PROCESS

When planning an interior space, you should utilize all the design data available to you. Begin by establishing the size of the task, including the scale of the design, the requirements of the client, the importance of any design features you feel should be included, and then the consequences of these. Once you have sketched out the scope of your project, try to assess the possibilities by eliminating any problems. It is important to weigh out the pros and cons in order to establish a strong conceptual approach to design considerations and decisions.

SKETCH DESIGN STAGE

List the priorities of the project to give yourself a strong starting point. These could indicate starting with a broad idea, such as creating a light and airy space, and then working toward defining more specifically what this may mean in terms of the design. Alternatively, you could focus on a specific idea from the outset, such as creating hidden storage systems. Exploring these will then help you to tackle the whole space. Whatever your starting point, you should begin with what matters most when responding to your planning.

Color is used as an architectural device, illustrating the possible uses of architectural components when they are added within the interior space.

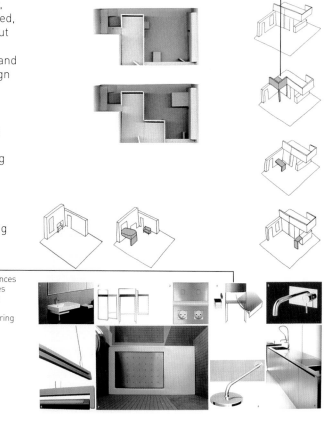

MODELS AND AXONOMETRICS

A series of axonometric drawings explore planning ideas for a residential space, while models help to test material relationships. By building up architectural components in an incremental fashion, the designer is quickly able to gauge the possible planning solutions for the design of an interior scheme.

Clear product references and material samples help to illustrate the look and feel of the intended scheme during the initial planning stages.

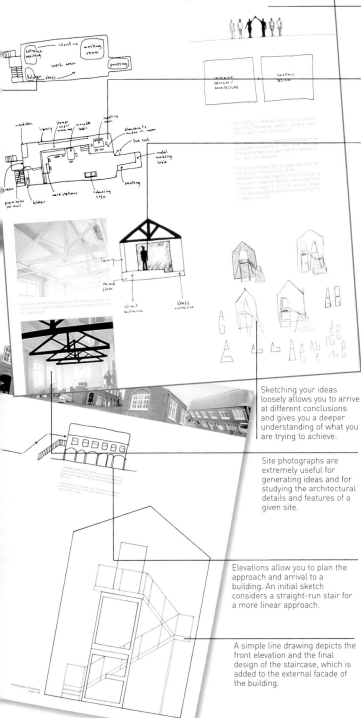

Creating a design proposal is vital for directing the design stages, and allows you to bring together and apply your project research to a given design scheme.

Diagrams are an excellent way to plan and brainstorm. Create sketch plans and notes to help you break down your design ideas and considerations.

A scaled figure in a sketch can highlight important ergonomic considerations when raising a floor or lowering a ceiling height.

Sketching your ideas loosely allows you to arrive at different conclusions and gives you a deeper understanding of what you are trying to achieve.

Site photographs are extremely useful for generating ideas and for studying the architectural details and features of a given site.

Elevations allow you to plan the approach and arrival to a building. An initial sketch considers a straight-run stair for a more linear approach.

A simple line drawing depicts the front elevation and the final design of the staircase, which is added to the external facade of the building.

PLANNING

A good way of defining the position of activities or different zones is to create a bubble diagram. This is a loose diagram that illustrates the position of spaces, as well as describing their size and ratio in relation to other spaces. For example, a practical area may be given a larger bubble in the diagram in relation to a non-functional area. You may want to connect or position these spaces next to each other in an attempt to show how one space flows into another. Spatial hierarchy is important when planning, and this reiterates the need to prioritize your design criteria.

PROJECT

Chose a space in your home that you would like to redesign. This can be either a functional, practical space such as a bathroom or a kitchen, or a relaxing space such as a lounge or bedroom. Choose a space that you think could benefit from improvement; this will provide you with the most challenges.

STAGE 1 Making the survey

Now survey this space and make a card model at a scale of either 1:20 or 1:50. Consider any features that will affect the design, such as the position of light sources, entrances, or circulation areas. Once you are aware of possible restrictions, consider whether these restrictions can be changed or whether you will work with them.

STAGE 2 Planning the space

Using your client profile from Unit 14 and your design proposal as set out in Unit 15, sketch plan the space. If you are creating a functional environment, you will need to decide on the position of the services and the way in which activities will be supported. If you are creating a relaxing environment, you may want to consider using the light sources to maximize views and light. Always alternate between drawing and modeling in order to develop your understanding of the physical and spatial qualities of your ideas.

STAGE 3 Preparing the client presentation

Once you are happy with the design, draw up your final plan, and create an axonometric or perspective view of the space. Render this drawing to illustrate the different materials and colors that you intend to use. Complete the project by providing a sample board of all the finishes, fixtures, fittings, lighting, and furniture that you have sourced.

CASE STUDY 05: Retail shop

THE BRIEF
To create a directional interior that reflects a contemporary attitude to fashion.
Budget: Small: the client is a boutique owner and fashion buyer who has a unique approach to fashion clothing.
Designers: Forster, Inc.

Fashion is big business. In a never-endingly competitive climate, fashion designers require equally stimulating environments to showcase their latest creations. The shop represents the threshold into the world of fashion, and the shop window creates the opportunity for us to glimpse this world. The following case study will examine the world of retail design and the importance of design and display. Having a ready-made product provides an excellent starting point for design language, and a vital end point for a design scheme.

DESIGN CONCEPT
The opportunity to collaborate with another designer is always interesting, enabling the designers to pool their resources and ideas together in a profitable exchange. In this case study, the design team was able to work alongside cutting-edge fashion labels, which inspired the concept of the design scheme. It was important to provide an exciting setting that would support the garments without detracting from them.

WINDOW FRAMING
The shop window serves as an exciting threshold between different interior and exterior worlds. Large bold typography is applied directly onto the shop window and sits neatly on the windowsill to keep the facade simple and understated. The name of the retail space frames the garments within.

USE OF LIGHTING
Clever lighting effects create accents and highlights. A skylight placed at the far end of the shop draws clients in toward the dressing and pay area. Adjustable lighting creates warm halos around clothes trees, and spotlights shine on the white polished concrete floor.

DESIGN STRATEGY

A key design consideration was the display of the garments, as well as the design of the necessary fixtures and fittings. Keeping the space entirely white, the designers were able to create display trees made from powder-coated steel tubes, and then position these as focal points in the space. Cleverly positioned full-length mirrors exaggerate the reflection of the trees to create a sense of a forest landscape. Each tree accommodates three different levels of hanging space to maximize the display of different garments.

The cashier's station is both functional and sculptural. Designed from fiberboard and sprayed white with a white laminate top, its shelves are stackable and flexible, according to staff requirements.

MATERIALS AND FINISHES

While keeping the interior as a white cube gallery, the designers wanted to play with a simple white color scheme, adding more texture and richness. One wall is clad with tongue-and-groove to give an undulating surface, while other walls are left with a simple plaster finish, painted white. Elsewhere, the use of paint finishes switches from gloss to matte in order to vary color effects and finishes. The changing room area is created from a hospital curtain rail with a simple plastic curtain. A clever softwood partition is clad with a white shag pile rug to add a different white texture to the interior while concealing shop stock behind. The final dramatic effect of white is played out in the floor, with a white polished concrete surface that acts as a pool of wet light. Halogen floodlighting above the display trees helps create a dramatic display of task and accent lighting. In this interior, shades of white and a mixture of textures provide a cool scheme as a backdrop to contemporary fashion labels for men and women.

ADVENTURES WITH MIRRORS

The illusion of a "fashion forest" is created by the position of mirrors, doubling the landscape of the interior to create playfulness and visual delight.

MAXIMIZING DISPLAY SPACE

Display fixtures are kept apart from the walls, increasing the depth of the interior by exploiting the height of the space. Powder-coated steel trees extend from floor to ceiling, providing three levels of hanging space. Garments are hung from branches at regular intervals for easy browsing.

A BLANK CANVAS

Lighting, textiles, and fabric create soft white zones for dressing areas. Free from color and clutter, they provide a perfect environment for trying on garments.

Mirrors are used above the cashier's station and around the trees to accentuate the interior, extending the feel of space and light.

The custom-made cashier's station is flexible in design, able to provide practical storage while still serving as an important aesthetic object to complement the interior.

CASE STUDY 06: Coffee house

THE BRIEF
To design a raw industrial shell and to create a brand identity for an existing chain of coffee houses.
Budget: Small to medium: the client is an entrepreneur with a chain of coffee houses.
Designers: Forster, Inc.

Commercial design requires a thorough understanding of many different and complex dynamics. The designer must consider both the client, who will be looking to make money, and the consumer, who will be looking to spend, while supporting the brand in such a way as to accommodate the ethos of the product. This case study illustrates a particular approach to the design of a commercial interior. Here, old and new design elements combine to create a rich design vocabulary. Architectural features inherited from an old site are successfully integrated with new design ideas, the outcome being a coffee house in a relaxing and eclectic style.

DESIGN ETHOS
The design team, which worked closely with the client on two other coffee house sites, approached each site as an opportunity to refresh, develop, and redefine the brand identity in such a way that it could then be applied to new locations. The sites were chosen both for their architectural character and for their position within the cultural quarter of the city. Envisioned as a meeting point for young professionals working in the creative industries, the coffee house provides an upbeat and quirky environment in which to relax.

A large sheet-glass facade reveals the double-height interior space, and creates panoramic views for both customers and pedestrians outside.

FIRST IMPRESSION
In keeping with the shell-like interior, the facade of the coffee house is very informal in character with its seeming lack of commercial identity. Free from exterior logos, the coffee house uses its interior space to advertise its own brand of relaxation, whether short- or long-stay.

DESIGN CONCEPT

The client was eager to preserve the raw and industrial character of the double height space, with a view to maximizing the range and number of seating positions within it.

A combination of second-hand sofas and chairs are mixed with custom-made tables and ledges to provide a cost-effective solution. The eclectic style is further reflected in materials and finishes within the space. Plastered surfaces sit alongside breeze blocks, and the patina of peeled paint remaining from the previous occupants provides a backdrop for dramatic lighting. The powder-coated steel star frames provide armatures for coffee cup lampshades. Exciting details add to the overall ambience, with 1-in. (25-mm) plywood tables laminated with colored laminate to give stripped zoning. To complete the look, a solid walnut block-work surface tops a cast concrete bar, forming a central design feature in the space.

Coffee-cup lampshades are visual and architectural elements that give a sense of the overall ceiling height, floating down from steel star frames to create a cozy ambience. When viewed from the exterior, they act as decorative elements behind the glass facade.

The service areas are planned with a generous amount of circulation space, maintaining a high degree of practicality and efficiency for employee requirements.

ORGANIZATION BY COLOR

Bright colors mark extra flat seating bays in the window for a simple solution to busy lunchtime or service periods, accommodating maximum numbers.

Exposed surfaces and textures give the interior a raw feel and provide a neutral backdrop for the quirky and eclectic style of furniture pieces.

SERVICE AREAS

A long service counter supports the cash register and the display of fresh cakes and pastries, as well as providing the main worktop for food and drink preparation. Behind the service counter, custom-built storage houses all food items, crockery, and cutlery, while the worktops hold the coffee machines and dispensers. Having specified exact requirements taken from other coffee house sites, the designers ensure comfort, practicality, and a good working environment for employees.

4 Building construction

Understanding the construction of architectural components is part of the designer's responsibility. Often the structural and non-structural decisions a designer makes are predetermined by factors such as planning regulations, budgets, and client needs as well as responding to the spatial qualities a site may suggest. This chapter covers the fundamental aspects of this process. Although in-depth knowledge is not required, most practicing designers will have a basic knowledge of construction, as well as understanding the material choices available to them.

Key skills covered in this chapter are organizational skills and information gathering.

Unit 17 | Building components (page 84)

17

Unit 18 | Building materials (page 90)

18

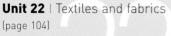

Unit 22 | Textiles and fabrics (page 104)

22

Unit 23 | Creating a directory (page 108)

23

See also
Unit 18: **Building materials** (page 90)

Unit 17: Building components

Floors, walls, windows, doors, and stairs are all architectural components. They help define our interior spaces by giving enclosure, division, and circulation, as well as providing shelter, warmth or coolness, and views. The design of internal components can vary, depending on the type of building and the layout of activities. This unit will review the construction and purpose of major building components.

FLOORS

The floor space defines the horizontal plane within the interior and is responsible for supporting live loads— such as the weight of people and furniture—as well as dead loads, including the weight of the floor construction itself. A timber floor is usually constructed by laying a series of linear joists on their short side. This gives maximum strength for overlaying with floorboards. A concrete floor can be cast in situ or by using pre-cast concrete planks on a steel joist floor. Floors that accommodate load movement must be relatively stiff but maintain elasticity. Floor loads are then transferred horizontally to beams, columns, and load-bearing walls.

The depth of the floor should relate to the scale and proportion of the structural span of the material, as well as the material's relative strength. The depth should also be considered when running electrical or mechanical lines parallel to beams under the floor system. With so many different choices of floor systems, designers should seek advice from a professional engineer to ensure the most effective floor solution.

LEADING THE EYE
A continuous floor material creates a spacious open-plan feel and allows the eye to travel along the space.

WALLS

Walls project vertically within interior spaces to provide planes of enclosure and division. Walls can be load-bearing (supporting loads from above) or partition (non-structural), to define different interior spaces. Either way, their construction should accommodate thermal insulation and acoustic separation, as well as supporting conduits for mechanical and electrical lines. Exterior walls are important for providing shelter from the elements, and their construction should control the movement of hot and cold air, as well as moisture and vapor. It is vital, therefore, that the exterior structure of a building is durable and able to resist weathering.

Interior stud walls are normally constructed by making a framework of wall studs that sit at regular intervals corresponding to the width and length of common sheathing materials. The studs carry their loads vertically, and the sheathing material—which is then attached to the studs—helps to keep this framework rigid. All electrical services and insulation can be housed within the stud wall frame. The wall can be finished in a variety of materials, the most common being drywall with a plaster finish, usually painted for a smooth, flat surface. In the case of more dense material constructions, such as masonry or concrete, walls tend to be designed with reinforcements to support tensile stresses. Height-to-width ratio is important in determining lateral stability and for controlling expansion with expansion joints.

CREATING A MOOD
The treatment of a wall surface can help define activities within a living space.

WINDOWS AND DOORS

These architectural components are most effective as framing devices for entrances and exits, for creating views within the interior, and for connecting the interior to the exterior. Doors give access between spaces, provide security and privacy, and help admit light and ventilate interior spaces. Windows allow us to gaze through the eyes of the building, letting in light and air, while shielding against noise and weather. The choice of products for both doors and windows varies according to the intended physical use and purpose, but manufacturers will provide standard sizes according to building regulations based on the requirements for door and window openings. Viewed from the exterior elevation, doors and windows are important for enhancing the architectural composition of the building's facade. The perception of the building will be affected by the position of such elements when they introduce contrasts in mass, scale, and transparency to the overall building form.

WINDOW TYPES

Windows, like doors, come in a variety of styles, including fixed, casement, sliding, double hung or sash, and pivoting types. Window frames can also vary in style, material, and construction to support glazing in wood, aluminum, or steel frames. Important factors which determine the choice of window type include the need for natural light and ventilation, sound, and thermal insulation, alongside cleaning and maintenance. Where possible, consult specialists to understand the different window types available.

DEFINING DETAILS
Period features, such as sash windows, accentuate the traditional proportions of the domestic interior.

ENLIGHTENED LAYOUT
Light sources help to articulate the layout of interior furniture.

SPACE GEOMETRY
The position of entrances, exits, and light sources gives a sense of interior geometry and circulation.

DOOR TYPES

Doors can vary in both their construction and their movement. Different types include swinging, sliding, folding, revolving, and pivoting doors, giving from 50 percent to 100 percent of opening to the doorway. Different styles include panel, sash, louver, French, and glass panel doors. Most choices depend on the location of the door in relation to its physical access requirements. Other factors include the envisioned movement between spaces, as well as the frequency of use or specific requirements such as light, ventilation, view, and acoustic considerations. The most important function a door can have is to prevent the spread of fire within a building. Fire-resistant doors can have standards that range from 30 minutes to 4 hours.

STAIRS

Stairs can be an important design feature in a building. A stair can affect the interior organization of spaces by influencing the structural system, and in some instances by determining the position of services within the overall layout. The role of the stair is to take you vertically from one level to the next. Within the context of a large building, stairs are particularly important for linking different parts of the building together, and for providing good overall circulation. The construction of stairs can be divided into two groups: either forming integral parts of the building structure, for example, concrete stairs, or components that are self-supporting, such as spiral stairs. Obvious safety considerations, when constructing a stair, must include comfort and ease of movement. This is largely determined by ergonomic data that give standards based on the proportions of the body and the movement of body parts.

STAIR TYPES

Other important considerations for the design of stairs include the provision of landings that are clear from obstruction and have a width and depth that equals the width of the stair. All stairs require a balustrade for comfort and safety. Stairs can vary in type according to functional requirements and space restrictions. They include straight run, L-shaped, curved, spiral, winding, 180-degree return, or U-shaped stairs.

LINKING SPACES
Whether internal or external, stairs are important for linking different parts of a building both physically and visually.

HEALTH AND SAFETY IN BUILDING CONSTRUCTION

Health and safety issues should be addressed during the design and construction stages, and cover both the duration of the job and the lifetime of the structure.

Safe working practices

A planning supervisor should be appointed (either a member of the design team or an external expert) to oversee the construction and coordinate site safety matters. He should have certified health and safety training and should ensure that the construction complies with construction codes and building regulations.

Building safety

A health and safety plan for the construction period should be prepared by the planning supervisor. A health and safety document should be given to the client on completion of the structure. The design team is legally obliged to foresee any risks, give priority to safe practices, and to avoid personal injury. Failure to comply with health and safety requirements could lead to criminal prosecution.

Building guidelines, regulations, and codes differ from state to state and country to country. When working abroad, designers should seek advice from local planning authorities and building construction organizations to ensure that they follow the necessary codes of practice in line with legislation.

FINISHES

The characteristics of any material are expressed by color, surface, finish, inherent pattern, weight, warmth, and response to light. These properties influence not only how it looks, but also how a material can be shaped, and how well it will perform and wear over time. The same material can have many different textures: stainless steel can be brushed to a matte or highly polished mirror-like finish. New forms of familiar products—such as stone and wood—are now available, and commercial materials such as concrete are increasingly commonplace in domestic interiors, providing seamless finishes.

WOOD

Ash, oiled

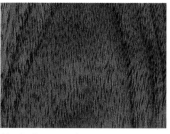
Maple, lacquered

Olive ash

Cherry, oiled

Maple, unfinished

American elm

Yellow pine

Red oak oiled

Yew

Siberian larch

CONCRETE

Acid-etched concrete

Polished plaster

Molded concrete

Combed concrete

STONE

Grisdevilette, acid washed

Lunel, polished

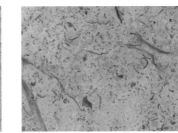

Frog eye limestone,

Broughton Moor slate, sanded

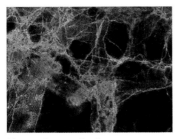

Marron Emperador limestone

Blue marble

Blue savoy marble

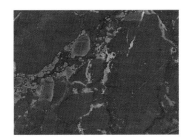

Brown marble

METAL

Stainless steel, relief

Stainless steel, stripe

Stainless steel, red embossed

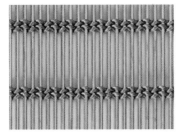

Wire, flexible weave

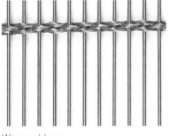

Wire and bars

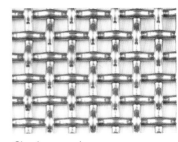

Stainless steel, blue embossed

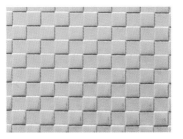

Chunky woven bars

Stainless steel, square relief

Unit 18: Building materials

OBJECTIVES
• Introduce the major building materials
• Understand the properties of building materials
• Learn to select materials

Designers enjoy working with materials, because these are the raw elements with which to bring a design idea to life. Whether you are trying to evoke an ambient interior or create a practical and functional environment, your choice of materials is key to achieving your ideas. This unit introduces some of the most prominently used building materials and their properties. The process of choosing a material may begin with an aesthetic appearance, but other factors include strength, durability, performance, and maintenance.

BUILDING WITH STRUCTURE

The primary function of building materials begins with structure. The purpose of a structure is to carry safely all loads imposed on the building to the ground, without collapsing under the load of the whole or its material parts. This is of concern to the interior designer when the design encompasses structural changes. Whether it is the construction of a stair, the removal of a wall, or the insertion of a mezzanine, the design and construction should provide strength and stability, as well as being fire resistant. This means complying with safety standards and ensuring the use of appropriate and suitable materials, so that structural integrity is maintained.

All structures are susceptible to tension and compression. These are natural forces, which result in materials either being pushed or pulled. Tension is created when a material is stretched or pulled. It is easy to recognize, because the material is lengthened in much the same way as a taut rubber band. Compression is the opposite of tension. When a material is compressed or pushed, it is shortened. A piece of foam will appear smaller when it is squashed. Structural materials are much stiffer than elastic or foam, so these effects are not readily detected to the eye, but they still occur. The strengths of wood, concrete, and steel vary in different degrees, yet all three materials are able to resist tension and compression before breaking under a load.

STRUCTURAL MATERIALS

Materials such as concrete (reinforced or pre-stressed), wood, steel, and aluminum are commonly used for building structures, and all have properties which make them effective for different building types and structures. The more strength a material has, the smaller the amount needed to resist a given load. As a general rule, framed structures that are tall and wide in span require materials that are strong and stiff under

BASIC CHARACTER
Timber is a beautiful natural material, creating a warm ambience.

MATERIAL PERFORMANCE
A glass facade is both dramatic and attractive. But it can also be high-maintenance, requiring regular cleaning.

pressure, but also light in weight. The relationship between the weight of a material and its strength gives an indication of its efficiency in its structural function, and is known as strength/weight ratio. A designer should try to achieve the most efficient method of building the structure to avoid cost and minimize material waste.

Wood

Wood is a beautiful natural material. It is available for building purposes in a variety of species, and can be broadly divided into two groups: softwoods and hardwoods. Softwoods, such as pine or spruce, are quick to grow and are relatively cheap, but wear more quickly than hardwoods. Their strength is relative to the presence of knots and faults, and the malleability of different structural softwoods. Hardwoods tend to be more expensive. Oak is the most diverse, and can vary enormously in color and texture. When compared to other materials, wood has low stiffness, but compared to its own light weight, it is relatively very stiff and therefore has a high strength/weight ratio. It is therefore a good structural material and can be used for beams, pillars, floors, and furniture, as well as covering ceilings and walls. It is a good decorative material when used to cover surfaces, especially in sheet form, and can be strengthened further with plastic glues to create plywood and laminated woods. Wood must be fire retarded even though this decreases its overall strength. The advantages of using wood as a building material is that it is easy to work with while being moderately strong in compression and tension and good for insulation. However, the use of wood in building construction is sometimes controversial for its ecological repercussions. Worldwide consumption of timber is occurring faster than it can be replaced. When buying wood, be sure to use an environmentally friendly source. Rare and exotic timbers, such as mahogany, teak, and iroko, can look stunning, but make sure that they are supplied by an environmentally managed forest.

Glass

Glass responds to the demands of safety, security, and thermal insulation while remaining decorative and practical. Its versatility allows it to be used in a wide range of domestic applications, including floor panels, partitions, screens, doors, windows, stair treads, shelves, and balustrades, as well as for lighting, splashbacks, and decorative surfaces. Glass technology has enabled it to be produced for structural and technical specifications in economically large formats of varying thicknesses. Although perceived as an aesthetic material, glass is surprisingly durable when toughened or laminated for domestic and commercial use. Glass partitions can provide separation, transparency, and privacy, Whether transparent, translucent, or opaque, there are limitless durable and decorative finishes, and an abundance of manufacturing techniques to choose from. Glass treatments can manipulate light, color, and pattern to make it functional and flexible, resolving many complex design requirements. Etched and sandblasted glass will gently diffuse light, according to pattern. Laminated glass with a colored inner layer will glow, while opaque floors shine once they are under-lit. Finishes include acid-etching, frosting, sandblasting, laminating, embossing, enameling, and tinting, as well as unusual glass finishes created from recycled low-waste products, such as televisions and car windows.

Steel

Steel is an alloy of iron and carbon. When a small amount of nickel is added, it becomes stainless steel, which does not rust. Its particular properties ensure that steel is a strong, stiff material, with a high strength/weight ratio. Steel is an economical material, because a small amount can carry a relatively large load. It comes in two types of strength: regular structural steel and high-strength steel. Its characteristics make it suitable for different kinds of building types, including both low- and high-rise structures, and effective for roof structures of all spans. The advantages of using steel as a building material relate mainly to its strength. Being one of the strongest materials in construction, steel is mostly used for suspension cables in bridges, trusses, and beams, for skyscraper columns, and for rollercoaster tracks. It is, however, susceptible to corrosion, and the cost of maintaining material surfaces is high. Steel requires regular painting and coating with a protective layer.

Concrete

Concrete, a man-made material, is a mixture of cement, sand, stone, and water. Its special material properties include plasticity, strength, and durability, making it attractive for its versatility. Concrete can be used in a variety of ways and for a number of purposes. It can be prefabricated, sculpted, or poured into various forms suitable to the channeling of loads. It is an excellent material for floors, walls, ceilings, and furniture, as well as for creating finishes. The strength of normal concrete can be varied according to its mix, depending on the ratio of water to cement, and cement to sand and stone. The finer and harder the aggregates (sand and stone), the stronger the concrete. The larger the amount of water, the weaker the concrete. Reinforced concrete, with steel bars, or pre-stressed with steel wires or cables, allows concrete to improve its performance under tension as well as compression. Concrete has many advantages as a building material. It is economic and cost-effective, fireproof, and weatherproof. It can be polished, painted, patterned, or kept rough to maintain its sculptural qualities

VISUAL QUALITIES
Materials can be exploited for their aesthetic properties such as texture, form, and color.

PHYSICAL QUALITIES
Structural materials need to be durable and strong if they are to perform well.

GREEN DESIGN

Ecological design strives to reduce material and construction waste by reusing or recycling products more efficiently. Strategies of sustainability can be embraced early on in the planning stages of the design by responding to alternatives. Strategies include reducing building where possible to be efficient, specifying those products or raw materials that are most efficient, substituting scarce resources for more plentiful ones, or reusing building materials from demolished buildings. Rehabilitating a site and its materials provides the designer with a real challenge, namely to transform an existing site into one which can accommodate new programs for new users. The advantages of recycling are evident when it comes to materials, but more interestingly, ecological design drives designers to be imaginative and innovative, and to respond with new ways of thinking. By reusing waste materials, architects and designers are creating new opportunities for their projects.

Building design

Clever building design can maximize solar energy gain, minimize heat loss, and optimize thermal efficiency and insulation. Strategic placing and orientation of light sources and reduction of large glazed areas are two examples of key design considerations.

Saving energy

Energy conservation can be achieved through carefully designed provision of services. For example, heat and power can be generated either with solar collectors or windmills—systems that do not produce carbon dioxide, and are economical to run. Energy can also be saved by reclaiming heat waste from cookers and refrigerators, and by reducing long pipe runs that waste heat. Domestic heating and hot water can be separated by giving each system its own controls. Natural ventilation or passive stack ventilation systems can be used instead of air conditioning to avoid excessive heat loss, and low-energy or high-frequency fluorescent lamps also save energy.

CONSERVATION
Solar panels help to maximize energy gain to generate heat and power for the home.

Water consumption

Leak detectors, flow regulators, and water recycling systems all help to avoid wastage. Rainwater can be collected, filtered through underground tanks, and pumped to points of use. Gray water from baths, showers, and basins can also be pumped to header tanks to be recycled back to WC and urinal cisterns. Home appliances with minimum water consumption are energy efficient, and cisterns with dual or low-volume flushing systems help to reduce water wastage.

Building materials

Green design should include materials that are of low embodied energy, which means all the energy used in their production and transportation. Using local materials helps to reduce pollution from transportation. Materials should be non-toxic and their production should not be harmful to the environment. Wood should be supplied by a Forest Stewardship Council (FSC) to ensure that the timber is from a sustainable and renewable source. Pre-treated timber is best as tighter controls are carried out under factory conditions. Alternatives to synthetic materials are plentiful and flooring is available in many renewable forms; either FSC-accredited wood, reclaimed timber, cork, coir, linoleum, or wool. Paints should be low in odor, non-toxic, solvent-free, and, ideally, water based.

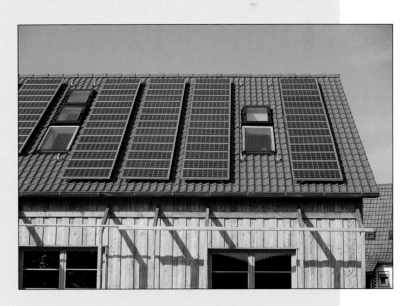

Unit 19: Services

OBJECTIVES
- Introduce utility services
- Understand the organization of utility services within buildings
- Learn to research different utility systems

The installation of utilities or useful services brings buildings to life by linking them to direct supplies of water, electricity, gas, and telecommunications. This unit will introduce important technical information regarding the organization and distribution of utility services within the domestic environment.

A building can be compared to a living body, with the distribution of services through pipes resembling arteries and telecommunications cables corresponding to nerves. It is important that the anatomy of the building is constructed with careful consideration being given to the installation of services in such a way as to help minimize and rationalize the route of supply—particularly water services to bathrooms and kitchens. Utility services commonly run through the building vertically through duct spaces, and horizontally under floor constructions and through the voids above suspended ceilings.

ROUTING CABLES
Cabling is routed through floors and walls in hidden horizontal and vertical runs.

WATER SUPPLY
Water is sourced both above ground, from streams and rivers, and below ground, once rainwater has permeated through the strata to form the water table. The urban supply system draws its water supply from large reservoirs, piped to the water mains under each street. In isolated areas, private wells are sunk to reach the water table from which water is then pumped up to the building's storage tank.

PURIFICATION
Before it is supplied, water is filtered to remove sediment, treated with chlorine to eliminate harmful bacteria, and softened with chemicals to remove hard-water salts. Excessive hardness in water can increase corrosion of the plumbing system, causing damage from scaling and furring.

DISTRIBUTION
Once connected to the main, each building needs access to water for drinking, cooking, cleaning, washing, and sanitation, as well as for heating and cooling systems and fire protection. Water reaches our homes through the operation of pressure, expressed in terms of head (the height to which the water in the main rises in a vertical pipe). This pressure is great enough to allow water to travel vertically through pipes to storage tanks and cisterns. A series of valves then controls the flow of water to each fixture, and also cuts off the supply to enable repair and maintenance.

DRAINAGE
In a domestic building, it is common to rationalize the design of bathrooms and kitchens by reducing the distribution of pipe runs for drainage, so that the supply is used economically and logically. Each sanitary appliance discharges through lateral runs (branches) into a main downward collecting pipe (stack). This is connected to an underground lateral run (drain), and this in turn to the public collecting sewer. Discharge from all appliances except the toilet is called waste and the liquid that comes from the toilet is called soil. Taking the waste and soil away requires pipes of suitable material, size, and progressive fall to the sewer.

ELECTRICITY SUPPLY

Electricity is vital for delivering power for many of the domestic services, including heat, light, appliances, security, and communications. As technologies become more sophisticated, the layout and installation of electrical services can adapt to provide more flexible systems. Hidden cabling runs are made either horizontally or vertically, for easy location and to help to reduce damage if rewiring is later required.

DISTRIBUTION

Electricity enters through cables below the ground, where it is fed through to a mains box and then distributed through a number of circuits to supply each space within the home. Each circuit is protected by its own specially rated fuse, meeting the power demands of individual heavy-loaded appliances, such as cookers and immersion heaters. Lighting circuits, which tend to be lightly loaded, require a simpler circuit form. The separation allows routing to be isolated for repair, and wiring for circuits to be sized according to its likely maximum load. Fuses protect each stage in the distribution hierarchy. The earth protects the user, ensuring that if a loose wire makes the outer casing of an appliance dangerously live, the fuse will blow and make the system safe.

SAFE PRACTICES

Switches allow an appliance to remain off while the source remains potentially live. For safety, bathroom switches are mounted outside the room and inside with an insulating length of pull-cord. Sockets for plumbed appliances are never mounted within reach, except for safety sockets designed for electric razors, which contain an isolating transformer. Specialists may be employed for the design and installation of electrical and electronic systems, but it is important that the designer is aware of the spatial,environmental, operation, and safety requirements.

HEALTH AND SAFETY

Always ensure that professionals are qualified, certified in health and safety training, and well protected on site.

GAS SUPPLY

Gas is the simplest utility service. The use of manufactured town gas composed from coal and oil has long since been surpassed by the use of natural gas, which is more directly derived from natural sources and mostly oil-related. Used in the US, the UK, and most of Europe, natural gas is the economical, easy-to-use method most often used for heating, cooking, etc.

DISTRIBUTION

The supply of gas is networked and piped from the regional grid and its installation within the home is similar to that of the water supply. Entry is usually at the lowest level. The sequence is stopcock, pressure governor, meter and then piped distribution. Internally 1-in. (25-mm) pipes are made of copper and reduce down to ½ in. (15 mm) depending on the appliance being supplied—boiler, cooker, water heater, or fire.

SAFE PRACTICES

Safety is paramount. Though modern gases are less toxic than old-style town gas, they still asphyxiate and emit carbon monoxide if incomplete combustion occurs in a faulty appliance. Supplies are not routed through bedrooms, as leaks can be fatal. Consequently, meters and pipes are never housed in unventilated cavities, so that if leaks do occur they may be detected easily.

HEATING, VENTILATION AND AIR CONDITIONING (HVAC)

The primary objective of HVAC systems is the comfort and practicality of environments to suit the needs of human activity by balancing indoor and outdoor conditions.

HEATING

The choice of energy source to distribute heat within a building—solid fuel, oil, gas, or electricity—can be based on amenity and economy. The choice of thermal installation should take into account the degree of control needed to produce good conditions, its appearance, position, maintenance, servicing, and how much it costs to install and run.

DISTRIBUTION

Heat can be distributed by direct heaters, electric heaters, boilers, or radiators. In central heating systems, fuel is converted to heat within a central plant; the heat is then distributed throughout the building by pipes and ducts. An effective system emits the maximum amount of heat for the minimum amount of material with the least cost of the material purchased. Water is generally the most efficient medium and the most widely used for its cost-efficiency.

VENTILATION AND AIR QUALITY

Ventilation provides a supply of oxygen and for the circulation of air to combat overheating, pollution, or smell. Natural ventilation is generally the responsibility of the designer and is normally met by windows and doors. In the absence of natural ventilation, mechanical ventilation or air conditioning is required.

DISTRIBUTION

In mechanical ventilation or air conditioning, the air is drawn in, exhausted by fans, and then distributed through a network of ducts. Air is heated in the winter and cooled in the summer. Effective air conditioning and mechanical ventilation systems should enable heat recovery.

SAFE PRACTICES

Where fumes and pollution are likely to be hazardous or cause environmental risks, they should be removed at the source by hoods or extractor fans.

See also
Unit 16: **Planning your design** (page 76)

Unit 20: Lighting

OBJECTIVES
- Learn to achieve different lighting effects
- Choose appropriate lighting products
- Learn to create a lighting plan

A good lighting scheme should strive to improve and enhance the interior and maximize the final design. Whether working, relaxing, or undertaking a particular task, all activities require light. A lighting scheme should identify all major activities that take place in the space to determine where the appropriate light sources should be placed.

Lighting is one of the most important elements in any interior, and the preparation for a successful solution must begin in the early stages of your design. Without power being supplied to the right places and some idea of how to achieve lighting effects, we may be disappointed with the result.

WHAT IS LIGHT?

All light sources, both natural and artificial, are made up of wavelengths of color—the colors of the spectrum. These combine to give white light. The varying quantities of these wavelengths can affect the color of the light itself, the color temperature, and the way in which the light allows us to see a color, which is color rendering. When considering any interior lighting scheme, it is important to have certain information regarding the light sources available and the impact they can have on your space.

LIGHTING PLAN

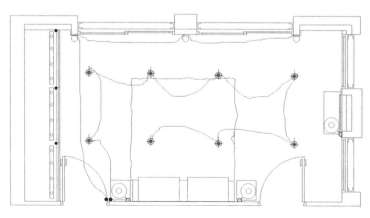

DIAGRAM CLARITY
A lighting plan illustrates the placement of lighting fixtures and their position in the room's electrical circuit.

USING SHAPE
The addition of this wall light continues the rectangular theme set up within the overall design.

KEY

Recessed 50W low-voltage units QR-CB51 lamps

Freestanding 5 amp circuits assumed 60–100W GLS lamps (client's selection)

Surface-mounted low-voltage wall lights

Surface-mounted inter cabinet units (to closets) 10W QTLP-ax lamps (door operated)

Wall-mounted switches

Switches for door-operated lights

SURFACE BRIGHTNESS AND REFLECTANCE

When planning a lighting scheme, you should take into account the surface colors within the space. Lighter, more reflective colors will both increase the light on surfaces and the level of light, whereas darker and less reflective surfaces will absorb light. This loss of light will reduce the perceived brightness of the space as compared to that of a lighter space with the same light fittings and lamp wattage. Color rendering refers to the way in which light affects the color of surfaces within a space, as well as its ability to distribute color.

LAMPS

When discussing lighting, the term "lamps" does not mean freestanding decorative products. Light bulbs are lamps. There is a wide range of lamps, available in many shapes and sizes. Artificial light sources and lamps are divided into groups, depending on how they produce light.

Incandescent

These lamps produce light as the power supplied causes the filament to heat and glow, or incandesce. They are widely used in North America and Northern Europe for residential lighting, so we are all familiar with the warm color appearance they provide. Natural daylight has full spectrum color, and all of the color wavelengths exist within it. Incandescent sources are the best choice of artificial light if the rendering of color is important. The disadvantages of these sources are their inefficiency and the comparatively short length of their life, as the filament gradually degrades over time until it finally breaks.

FREESTYLE ILLUMINATIONS
Freestanding lamps offer light in specific areas of a space, adding to the decorative style.

INTRODUCING COLOR
Lighting can be used to enhance and even create color within a neutral material color scheme.

Fluorescent

Light is produced within fluorescent lamps when the electricity supplied reacts with the phosphor coating on the inside of the lamps. The quantity and type of the phosphor coatings also affects the color temperature and the color rendering of fluorescent lamps. Fluorescent lamps can be selected in a variety of types to suit different lighting applications. They are more efficient than incandescent lamps.

Halogen lamps

Halogen lamps are a type of incandescent light source in which the passage of current through a filament raises its temperature until it produces light through incandescence. In all incandescent lamps the filament is contained within a vacuum where the addition of an inert gas reduces the rate at which the filament particles evaporate and so optimizes the lamp life. Halogen lamps have iodine or bromide added to the vacuum, causing the filament to burn more brightly but reducing the evaporation of the filament particles. Low-voltage (12-volt) halogen lamps have a thicker and shorter filament, creating a brighter, more intense light than 240-volt versions as the filaments have a greater surface area.

HID—high intensity discharge

Discharge lamps produce light by passing current through a number of gases or vapors. With no filaments to deteriorate, they have a longer lamp life and are very efficient because they consume less power than filament sources to produce a similar light output. The type and pressure of the gas vapor defines both the color temperature and color rendering of the lamps. Lamps with sodium under low pressure produce the yellow light source used for street lighting, whereas lamps with mercury under high pressure are used where the light needs to be whiter and render more accurately subtleties of color.

Others

In addition to the most widely used types, there are certain lamps that produce light as electricity reacts with gases inside the glass envelope—these are known as discharge lamps. Other types, which produce light using a magnetic current, are known as inductive lamps. Both types feature in lighting schemes where efficiency and long lamp life are important issues. They are rarely used in residential lighting.

BEDROOM FUN
These floor-mounted LED uplights add a gentle brightness with a touch of color.

LEDs and fiber optics

These deliver light into a space in different ways, but share the advantages of being cool to the touch and needing relatively low maintenance. This gives the opportunity to provide light in places where it would be difficult to use other types of lamp.

Is it all about brightness?

Light is measured in a unit called a lux, and we can find out how much light there is in a space by calculating the lux level. Although this gives us a numerical value, it often doesn't really tell us what the lighting will look like. In addition, brightness is a subjective term and its perception varies from person to person. Quite often lighting schemes are designed based on a grid of lights in the ceiling, delivering a uniform amount of light across the space. This does not consider elements such as the furniture layout, artwork, or architectural features, and as a result atmosphere is lost. It is a valuable exercise to observe lighting schemes in spaces you enjoy. Try to see how the lighting has been positioned, and note how it has been used to enhance the various elements.

Introducing flexibility

Uniform brightness may not be the answer, but it may be important sometimes. Every room should be assessed, and the provision of lighting for each particular activity should be introduced. Consider working, relaxing, playing, and eating, noting where they will take place and how you want them to be lit. It is likely that most rooms will need lighting that allows for a number of activities. Several lighting circuits will allow for the light to be switched to suit the different activities, changing the amount of light and its position.

Presenting your ideas

Lighting effects can be difficult to demonstrate. It is possible to create virtual images, but they can be time-consuming to produce unless you are a specialist. Think about collecting images of your favorite effects to use on a lighting concept board so that you can show your ideas. The positions of light fittings and circuits can be shown on a lighting plan (see page 96). This is a simply prepared drawing, using symbols explained in a key to denote each product type. The symbols are then looped together to denote individual circuits.

THE PROJECT

Evaluating the lighting in your own home is a good way of getting to know how lighting affects the way you enjoy the spaces you live with.

The process

Take a look at two rooms in your home, and list all the activities that take place within them. It would be good to pick one room that is generally quite busy, such as a kitchen, and one that is used for relaxation, such as a lounge or a bedroom. How many different lighting scenes are available within this space? Do you think that you have enough lighting flexibility to suit the different activities? Consider the layout of the space and the positioning of furniture.

The outcome

For each room, make a list of the lighting sources and positions that you think are suited to the space, and the ones that you would consider changing. Draft out a sketch lighting plan, and make a sample board to illustrate your choice of different products and their specifications.

VERSATILE DESIGN
Lighting need not always come from above. Think about the effect of light from different angles.

See also
Unit 04: **Developing an idea** (page 24)

Unit 21: Color and interiors

OBJECTIVES
- Introduce basic color theory
- Understand color terminology
- Learn to create a color scheme

Imagine a world without color. Color is more than just an aesthetic tool—it is vital for providing information about our environments, as well as helping us to navigate around them. Applied color in the field of interior design can be used practically, decoratively, and architecturally, giving a sense of place and identity. The interior designer can shape the environmental field by considering color at the outset of the design process. This unit introduces you to basic color theory and terminology. The use of color harmony integrates color as one of the main design constituents for transforming interior spaces and schemes.

COLOR WHEEL
The color wheel is an invaluable tool. The bands of color—red, orange, yellow, green, blue, and violet—are arranged in a segmented circle to show their relationships. Use it to understand the concept of the primary, secondary, and tertiary colors, as well as complementary and harmonious color juxtapositions

When choosing textiles or paints for an interior scheme, remember that color can be an important tool to shape and alter space. It can make objects look lighter or heavier, spaces seem warmer or cooler, or cause planes to advance or recede. Generally, warm colors, such as red and yellow, tend to be advancing (making walls, for example, appear to come closer), while cool colors, such as blue and green, are receding. Brightness or intensity is a major factor in determining whether colors advance or recede. A very bright color is advancing and a dull warm one is receding. Although generalizations can be made, color is primarily subjective, relying on personal preference and on our sense of aesthetic well being.

COLOR THEORY AND TERMINOLOGY

Different colors can be created by mixing the three primary colors—red, yellow, and blue. A simple mix of primaries produces the secondary colors—orange (red-yellow), green (yellow-blue), and violet or purple (blue-red). Once a primary is mixed with a secondary, it becomes a tertiary color: red-orange or blue-green. The three primary colors have the three secondaries as their complementary opposites (green versus red, violet versus yellow, and orange versus blue).

Hue is the term used to distinguish one color from another: red from orange, for example, or orange from yellow. A particular red will be of a specific hue; it can thus be a bluer red, yellow-red, or pale or dark. Normally, the human eye can differentiate between millions of different hues. Value or tone is the term used to distinguish the apparent lightness or darkness of a color. For example, light blue is a color of high value, whereas navy blue is a color of low value. The black or white content of a neutral gray could also be described in terms of value. Chroma or saturation refers to the strength or the relative purity of a color, sometimes called intensity, purity, or colorfulness. Colors of strong chroma are those that approach the likeness of pure hues.

This interior illustrates the use of both primary and secondary colors for maximum contrast and visual stimulation.

COLOR HARMONIES

Color harmonies can be described simply as specific color ranges. They are used to balance colors so that combinations of these colors are harmonious or aesthetically pleasing. By following simple rules, color harmony can be utilized to create a successful interior color scheme.

CONTRAST

Color contrasts offer a high degree of visual stimulation. By moving away from the security of related harmonies, accent colors are used to emphasize a group of related colors by contrasting with them. Accent colors are complementary hues, found directly opposite the chosen colors on the color wheel. The complementary color is then introduced into the scheme in small amounts to provide a heightened color sensation. The overall effect serves to create a visual experience, in which both related colors and accent hues are intensified.

MONOCHROME

This color harmony is most prominently found in nature, within the extensive shades of green foliage. Monochromatic harmony is one-hue harmony, which combines colors derived from a color range of a single hue. These schemes have qualities that can either be warm or cool, yet they are not strictly neutral. They tend to be comfortable and relaxing, because they blend well with most lighting conditions. Monochromatic schemes can be further cooled with the addition of neutrals, such as white, gray, and black.

COMPLEMENTARY

The complementary color harmony provides a greater contrast within harmony by using complementary pairs. By employing high-contrast schemes, the designer can exploit the strengths and tones of two colors on opposite sides of the color wheel, such as red and green. For an effective high-contrast scheme, tone down one or all of the colors, or separate them with a related color or with neutrals, such as gray or white. Varying the amounts of complementary color, as well as their individual strengths, can result in successful design. Balance is the key. Above all, make sure that no individual color becomes dominant in the overall scheme.

THE PROJECT

Using a range of samples, apply color theory to your fabrics by creating three different color schemes. You should be adventurous with your choice of textures and fibers to make the most out of this exercise.

The process

From the samples you have gathered in your directory, start by dividing the colors into three different color harmonies—monochrome, contrast, and complementary. Once you are satisfied with the groups, source interior images that correspond to your color scheme.

The outcome

Present your final color schemes on an A2 (16.54 x 23.39 in.) board, and illustrate these with the found interior images. Make notes alongside the samples and images to keep as a valuable resource for a potential client. Remember, showing your work to a friend or colleague will help you gauge its effectiveness at the presentation stage.

THE MUNSELL COLOR SYSTEM

Albert Munsell's color notation system was first published in 1915 and is the one most widely used color system for reproducing color throughout the world. Since Munsell's death in 1918, the Munsell Color Company continues to produce color charts, slides, and color standards used by the creative industries and also within the study of geology, archaeology, and biology. Applied to the field of interior design, Munsell's color notation allows designers to describe and understand color accurately and precisely by the three dimensions of hue, value, and chroma.

Hue

Hue is the measurement of color around a circle defined by Munsell as "the quality by which we distinguish one color from another as a red from a yellow, a green, a blue, or a purple." This first dimension refers to where a hue sits in the spectrum of colors, but does not tell us whether the color is light or dark, strong or weak. The Munsell system is based on a ten-hue color circle, the five principle hues being red, yellow, green, blue and purple with five intermediary hues between each of these.

Value

Value is the measurement of color up a vertical pole and according to Munsell is "the quality by which we distinguish a light color from a dark one." The scale of value is conceived of as a vertical pole. At the bottom of the pole black represents the absence of light, while at the top white represents pure light. Between these two poles of black and white lies the division and gradation of grays. In everyday language, value is usually referred to as tone, with a low value indicating a dark color (such as a shade), while a high value would determine a light color (such as a tint).

Chroma

Chroma is the measurement of color radiating out on a horizontal axis away from a vertical pole. While a color may be described in terms of its hue as blue or green, or indicated by its value as light or dark, it is not described completely until the third dimension is included. The chroma refers to the strength or saturation of a given color—whether the color is intense and pure, or gray and lacking color. Colors differ in their chroma strengths with some colors being more powerful than others. The balance or harmony of color resides in the principle that all colors do not reach their maximum chroma strength at the same level of value. Red is twice as strong in chroma as blue-green, and consequently requires a greater number of steps to reach gray. Purple-blue reaches its maximum chroma at the fourth step of value, while yellow reaches its maximum at the seventh step.

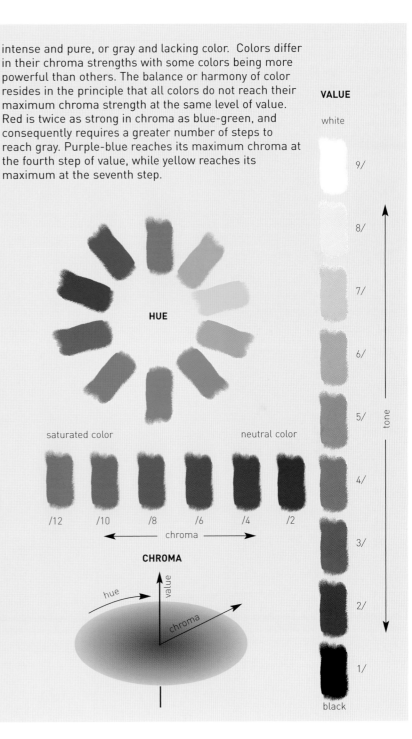

Unit 22: Textiles and fabrics

Textiles are one of the most versatile aspects of an interior. Designers are now taking advantage of new technology to use a wealth of striking and unusual textured fabrics within their spaces. Whether classical or contemporary in design, textiles combine fiber, color, and texture to create bold weaves, soft silks, and jumbo felts. This unit explores the application of textiles and fabrics within interior design, combining aesthetics, utility, and durability.

Fabrics are extremely important when it comes to defining the character of an interior scheme. They can be used to highlight and accent the qualities of a given space in order to enhance a company's corporate identity, give character to retail branding, or simply add comfort and harmony to the home. With such an extensive range of fibers, styles, and colors, a designer can find an array of fabric choices. Strongly linked to fashion, manufacturers are constantly updating ranges and launching new series and styles. It is imperative, therefore, that designers are aware of the fabric choices available to them.

NATURAL AND MIXED FIBERS

Cotton, silk, and wool are all associated with subdued colors and delicate natural finishes, providing an informal appearance for a variety of interiors. Natural fabrics are pleasing, because they appear raw, unrefined, and formal in their material qualities. Technology has developed fiber mixes that produce more durable textiles for the home in a wide range of weights and finishes. Fiber mixes have transformed textiles, changing cotton into linen, denim, muslin, or chenille, and wool into tweed or cashmere. Silk is luxurious to touch, but is also the most fragile. Mixing silk with cotton offers greater durability. While irregularities in natural fibers are part of their richness, fabrics made from mixes of man-made and natural fibers are generally sturdier and more durable than fabrics made from natural fibers alone, and can be more cost-effective. When buying patterned or repeated textiles, designers should obtain a good-sized sample to view before buying a larger amount. The standard widths of natural fabrics depend upon the manufacturer. Surface textures can vary according to the fiber and weave. Mixtures of either natural or synthetic fibers are generally used within the residential sector and in commercial design for upholstery and drapes, soft furnishings, and screens.

Wool and nylon

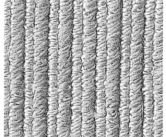
Linen

Mixed fibers

Mixed fibers

UTILITY

Utility fabrics are a good choice for upholstery as they are more resistant to wear and tear, and are generally more durable than other types. Fabrics are available in a wide range of colors and finishes, including heavy woven cottons, canvas, and Teflon-coated fabrics, which are extremely durable and soil-resistant. Commercial fabrics are generally described by the amount of rubs they can take—this refers to the process of fabric being mechanically rubbed to ascertain its durability. These fabrics are often pre-treated for stains and are resistant to tears, creasing, heat, flame, and even UV rays.

Denim

Tyvek

Canvas

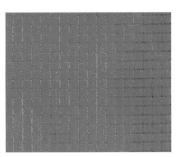

Ripstock

Hemp

Hessian

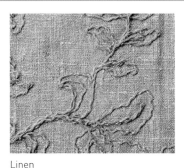

Linen

Cotton

Silk

Muslin

Cotton

Cotton

Jute

Jacquard

LUXURY

Modern and traditional
manufacturing methods have
combined to offer a range of
tactile and luxurious fabrics—
raw silk, velvets, and chenilles,
as well as unusual mixes, such
as wool mohair and silk voile.
Designers now have a choice
between traditional but delicate
fabrics, such as silk taffetas,
and more hardwearing but
equally glamorous synthetics.
Manufacturers can provide
fabric to specific requirements
and offer complementary wall
coverings, together with a
range of detailed trimmings.
The demand for luxurious
fabrics has ensured that silks,
velvets, and chenilles are
available at affordable prices,
but manufactured blends
(viscose, polyester, acrylic, and
acetate) offer equivalent options
that are cheaper and more
practical. Luxury fabrics are
used in almost every
environment to communicate
aesthetic values and
comfortable indulgence.

Mohair

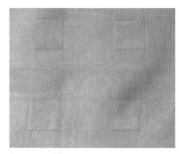
Chenille

Organza silk

Gold quilt

Cotton and silk

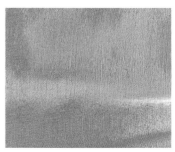
Metal silk

Cotton and silk

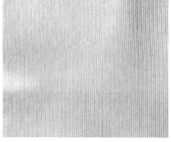
Ottoman

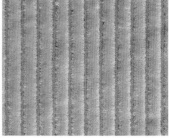
Jumbo corduroy

Silk

Silk

Handwoven silk

LAYERS

Lace or sheer curtains have been traditionally used to filter light while providing privacy. Contemporary materials have enabled designers to replace conventional choices with delicate layered organzas, lightly textured subtle sheers, and detailed laser-cut fabrics. These fabrics provide the same sheer qualities, contrasting matte and shine, transparency and translucency to increase the depth of the interior. Alternatively, chunky folds, pleats, or creased and crushed felts can provide bold thresholds and colors to divide and zone interior spaces. Creating fabric panels or walls is an economical way of covering storage areas or breaking up large spaces. Whereas a solid partition would dramatically make a space feel smaller, fabric divisions provide a visual threshold that can allow a space to remain light and airy while maintaining a degree of separation and seclusion.

Lace

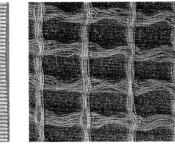

Sheer

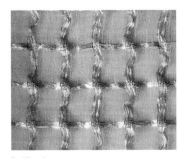

Raffia sheer

Felt appliqué

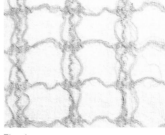

Fine layer

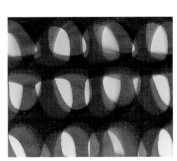

Three-layered sheer

Viscose and polyester

Viscose and cotton

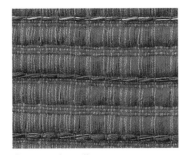

Cotton and acrylic

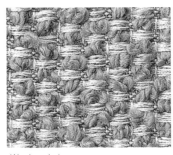

Wool and viscose

MODERN SYNTHETICS

Modern technology has enabled manufacturers to combine innovation with durability and functionalism. Alongside printing processes, machines can now smooth out irregularities and manipulate fibers into a variety of weights, mixes, and finishes. Industrial playfulness has revitalized the role of synthetics. Often scorned as cheap and nasty, modern synthetic fibers such as acrylic, viscose, and polyester have been reintroduced for their interesting surface qualities as well as their practical benefits, such as resistance to stains and fire. Improving their performance has not been at the expense of appearance—good-quality synthetic mixes are hard to distinguish from silks.

Unit 23: Creating a directory

A lot of legwork goes into researching and specifying products, materials, and services. Keeping up to date and being aware of recent design developments entails amassing a huge amount of product literature and samples, as well as keeping a record of important contact details. Creating your personal directory of products and services will enable you to organize your resources quickly and efficiently, ensuring that you have a valuable archive of references at your fingertips.

Most of your work in the latter stages of the design process will involve specifying and ordering products and services. The client will need to know what they are paying for, so product literature and material samples should be prepared well in advance. Be ready to offer other options if the material choices that you make do not appeal to the client. Whether it is floor coverings, light fixtures, or door furniture, it is a good idea to have more than one product handy at a presentation, even though the full range may not be offered up in the first instance.

In order to begin your directory, start collecting as much information as possible. Once you have gathered enough material, you can sort these out into a comprehensive system, illustrated by the following stages. This will be your most valuable resource when you come to write your client specification.

VISUAL REFERENCE
Illustrations and references are important when specifying particular finishes or features.

COLOR PALETTE
Swatches and paint samples are used to select color schemes or create color harmonies.

DIRECTORY CHECKLIST

Address book Keep an address book for all those useful names and numbers. Trial and error—as well as word of mouth—will allow you to build up good contacts within the industry. Separate different products under headings such as flooring, lighting, carpentry, joinery, paints, soft furnishing, furniture, fixtures, and electrical goods. Provide full details and contact names where possible.

Product literature File product literature under the same headings in lever arch binders (notebooks with a clamp inside instead of rings). Make sure to keep your information up to date by visiting trade fairs or by regularly requesting new literature from suppliers.

Samples Store fabric and other samples in box files and label these with a similar system so that you can find the corresponding catalog for the sample. Many of your samples will be used on sample boards, so make sure that these are replaced regularly.

Magazines Collect trade magazines and journals to archive in magazine files. These should be kept as reference materials and are extremely useful for generating ideas at the preliminary stage of product selection. If you wish to apply any of these references to boards, it is a good idea to make color copies of images, leaving your archive intact. There may be more than one project that requires the same reference.

FILING
Keep samples stored away in box files and ensure that they are labeled for easy access.

SOURCING SAMPLES
Metal, wood, stone, and laminate finishes are available in sample sizes from suppliers.

See also
Unit 16: **Planning your design** (page 76)
Unit 17: **Building components** (page 84)
Unit 18: **Building materials** (page 90)
Unit 19: **Services** (page 94)
Unit 20: **Lighting** (page 96)
Unit 23: **Creating a directory** (page 108)

Unit 24: Writing a specification

OBJECTIVES
- Learn to write a specification
- Choose appropriate products and materials
- Work to client requirements

As you might suppose, the word "specification" entails being specific. Having gained approval of your design proposals from the client, the next stage is to specify in writing the detail of every aspect of the work that is to be carried out. This specification forms a contract between you, your client, and the contractor. This unit will introduce you to writing a specification and clarify the do's and don'ts.

COMPREHENSIVE SPECIFICATION
Illustrate all the products together with the plan layout, identifying where these will go. Make a formal presentation to the client to approve the contract, making sure that the client understands the cost implications of the design.

Writing a specification is bound to raise issues that require clarification with the client before the specification can be issued to contractors for bids. It is essential to be thorough at this stage of preparing the specification because any missing requirements or details will incur additional costs for the client and may delay work on-site. While there is no definitive way of compiling a specification (the requirements and therefore the specification will vary with each project), it is important to establish a checklist as you think through the process. The accuracy and competence with which you write your specifications will improve with experience. Always be methodical and keep past specifications for reference.

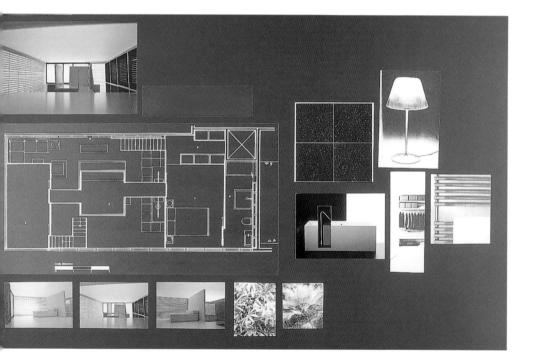

STAGE 1
Use the discussion notes taken with the client to break the project down into work stages. These stages need to take into account every room or area within the building in which changes are to be made. Start with what is existing and proceed to list the work that needs to be implemented until the spaces are finished. Categorize these into the appropriate headings for each space, such as preparation, strip out, scope of work, services, finishes, joinery, decoration, fixtures, fittings, and electrical.

STAGE 2
Whether you are dealing with builders, plumbers, and electricians, or organizing painters and decorators, you will need to specify the work to be carried out as well as decide who will do it. Divide the headings accordingly, so that construction work may be one specification, for example, while furnishings will be another.

STAGE 3

Make sure that each specification is headed with the following paragraphs (as applicable or adapted) to ensure that the work is covered by the appropriate standard:

"All work is to be carried out to appropriate standards. This is intended to assume the best practices, in accordance with appropriate ICC and applicable local standards, are adopted."

"To ensure a smooth continuity of work, avoiding disruption and duplication, contractor to advise on schedule and discuss with supervising officer, advising of latest dates by which, either materials to be supplied by supervising officer or instructions to be issued to contractor by supervising officer."

"It is the contractor's responsibility to ensure the site is kept secure and neat at all times and that on completion of the specified work, it is left in a condition appropriate to the commencement of decoration."

"Do not scale. All dimensions to be checked on site. Any discrepancies should be reported to the designer or architect."

HOW IT WILL LOOK
Use interior images and catalog references to indicate color schemes, material finishes, and product features where possible.

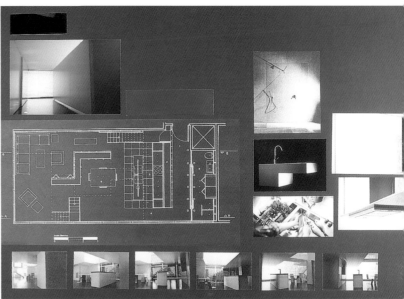

PROFESSIONAL PRESENTATION
A professional and well-presented scheme will inspire confidence from your client and will foster good working relations throughout the lifetime of the job.

CHANGES TO THE SPECIFICATION

Once the specification has been approved, any further changes and cost implications should be approved in writing and signed off by the client. It is advisable that any discussions with the client should be recorded throughout the lifetime of the job. Taking notes provides you with a good reminder of all that has been discussed, and allows you to highlight and prioritize important issues. Send a copy of your transcript in letter form to the client. This will confirm your discussion, and act as a further check to ensure that you have understood the issues correctly.

See also
Unit 17: **Building components** (page 84)
Unit 18: **Building materials** (page 90)
Unit 20: **Lighting** (page 96)
Unit 21: **Color and interiors** (page 100)

Unit 25: Creating a sample board

OBJECTIVES
- Learn to source products and samples
- Learn to prepare a sample board
- Understand how to present a final scheme

A sample board can evoke the mood and atmosphere of a final scheme by bringing together all your material choices on one presentation board. Details of materials, finishes, and products provide an exciting glimpse of what the finished design will feel like. Learn to select and source materials to create a sample board. This unit will give the guidelines for choosing the best way of presenting your chosen design.

CONTEXTUALIZING SAMPLES
Samples are displayed with illustrations to show how the interior will look as well as how it will function.

A sample board is a creative opportunity to put your design ideas into their context. With so many possibilities and decisions to make, you will need to focus on pulling your ideas together. An effective presentation of your materials will help you to conjure up the envisioned design scheme.

Start by considering the treatment of floors, walls, stairs, and ceilings. These are major elements within the interior setting and should be tackled first. Color, texture, light, and form should all be taken into account when developing the feel of the interior space. Remember that the relationships created between each material should encompass the overall concept for the space. Keep notes of your material choices, and provide reasons for these choices. To further your ideas for the space, collect references and images that illustrate the spatial properties you wish to achieve. This is particularly helpful when discussing potential ideas with the client. Design is a visual language and you should always have visual references that express your ideas. Try to avoid loaded images, such as advertising or lifestyle images. These are ready-made images that can contain messages or narratives that do not belong to you! Opt for simple architectural imagery that refers more specifically to the quality of spaces you wish to achieve.

The next stage is to imagine how you will light the interior shell effectively. Use lighting that will benefit the scheme architecturally. Research the market for different types and specifications. Consult lighting companies; show them your brief, and explain the effects you want to create within the design. This is a very good way of building up potential contacts within the industry, as well as getting you accustomed to the job of the designer. For detailing the design, consider all furniture, fixtures, and fittings. Your choice of products should be in context with the material setting you have created.

THE PROJECT

Following the guidelines given above, create a sample board for a domestic living space or for a commercial office environment. Choose a space that you can access and respond to the physical properties of the interior. With the domestic environment, decide what changes can be made, using different materials to enhance the space. If you have chosen an office environment, try to update and refurbish the existing company environment by providing new proposals for furniture, storage, and lighting.

The process

Create a posterboard-size sample board, illustrating the feel of your interior scheme with reference images, material samples, lighting, and furniture product images you have specified. Group the samples and images into their relevant categories when mounting; for example, lighting, furniture, walls, flooring, and so on. Include labels for products and text to explain the overall concept for the space. Present your sample board to a friend (playing the role of the client) for feedback.

LINEAR PRESENTATION

Materials and references can be archived simply on the presentation board as linear elements of information.

IMPRESSIONISTIC PRESENTATION
A creative montage doubles up as a sample board to express the material qualities of the interior.

PURE SAMPLES
A minimalist sample board keeps materials free from unwanted imagery, projecting pure physical qualities.

CASE STUDY 07: Large-scale residence

THE BRIEF
To expand the home for a new partner, with extra storage and custom furniture pieces for ultimate living solutions.
Budget: Good: the client is a banker in the city with a new love interest.
Designers: Forster, Inc.

Simple needs and practical requirements are the starting point for this large-scale desirable warehouse apartment. Storage becomes the driving force behind a good functional response to the brief. This case study illustrates that a project can work on many levels while creating an ergonomic and highly durable environment for living.

WEDGE STORAGE
A practical problem may be all that's required to inspire a creative and inventive design solution. The need for more storage is the turning point for this warehouse apartment, originally occupied by a single banker, and now transformed to accommodate a lifestyle for two. Two pieces were designed to fit from floor to ceiling in rooms 11 ft (3.3 m) high. Positioned near the entrance, the first wedge piece creates a secondary foyer within the main living area, while in the bedroom the slab neatly fits around the entrance to the en suite bathroom.

Dark walnut veneer is sandwiched between cream plastic laminate materials at the top of the slab and yellow strip lighting at the bottom.

SEPARATION OF SPACE
Storage in the bedroom uses dead space around the entrance to create a deep threshold between relaxation and washing. Fitted with dimmable florescent lights, a yellow glow permeates from below the slab to lift it slightly above the floor.

NEAT UPHOLSTERY
Upholstered surfaces define seating areas in chocolate brown leather to complement dark walnut wood. Hard and soft surfaces meet to create a flat and flush finish.

DESIGN DETAIL
The cabinet shell and shelves are constructed from MDF, and fitted with doors finished in ¾ in. (18 mm) birch ply. Vertical slabs are constructed from ¾ in. (18 mm) MDF, laminated with American black walnut veneer and cream plastic laminate. Seating pads are upholstered in brown leather, and accent lighting is provided with low-voltage downlighters and dimmable fluorescents. All wood surfaces are finished with clear wax oil.

ALL-PURPOSE STORAGE
Wedge storage systems create both exposed and hidden storage areas for display and concealment of clutter.

FIRST IMPRESSIONS
Linear elements are slotted, fitted, or inserted to create storage, division, and display. By the entrance, it creates a secondary foyer to frame the point of arrival and provides a clear threshold to the living space.

MULTIFUNCTIONAL UNIT
Based on straight lines and clean geometries, the wedge responds to the style of the warehouse apartment while maintaining its unique and individual identity as a piece of aesthetic furniture. It creates contrasts in color, texture, surface finish, and function to enhance daily domestic living.

CUSTOM FURNITURE

To complement the wedge storage, the designers were able to create a family of furniture pieces designed for home entertainment and containment. These included a drink box, TV box, and sound system box. The custom pieces are designed to be discreet and practical, drawing upon different influences such as geometry, puzzles, and Chinese lacquered boxes. The boxes are simple slabs, which hint at their function with changes of surface material, opening up to reveal the hardware within. Constructed using Buffalo board—a common ply sheet material used to line the interior of trucks—the surface of each piece was textured on one face and smooth on the other. Further details include acrylic Prada-esque tabs, with stainless steel push latches and magnetic fittings. Given a clear and functional brief, the design team was able to respond to the client, encompassing current trends with innovative and accessible design.

STREAMLINING
When closed, the furniture pieces are flush in appearance, with discreet changes in surface materials to help locate the position of the hidden storage compartments.

FUNCTIONAL DETAILS
Storage pieces have sculpted details and are tailored specifically to the users' home requirements to contain both entertainment hardware and electrical cables.

FLEXIBILITY
Furniture pieces can be placed vertically or horizontally. Storage areas are accessed by pushing magnetic doors to release steel latches. Opening in a series of combinations either up, down, sideways, or as drawers, flexibility creates the aesthetic look of this well-designed object.

STORAGE UNITS
A family of furniture pieces are slick, neat, and compact in design responding to the storage needs for stereo, television, and drink service. Streamlined for functionality and practicality, the pieces provide new storage solutions for domestic entertainment.

Stylish acrylic tabs provide detail for corners, edges, and junctions where materials meet. Constructed from Buffalo board, the surfaces of pieces are highly tactile.

CASE STUDY 08: Living as an event

THE BRIEF
To create an imaginative and contemporary space for living, which transforms everyday practicality into an aesthetic luxury.
Budget: Large: the client is a history lecturer.
Designers: Procter-Rihl

Once in a while, designers emerge to challenge conventional notions about the way we should or could live, offering new ideas, if we are prepared to start from scratch. In this particular case study, two architects with big ideas set out to build a house that explores every activity in the home, transforming each into an aesthetic and luxurious experience. Light, space, and the clever use of materials inspire a new kind of engagement with the home.

DESIGN STRATEGY

With an extremely linear site, nestled in a conservative neighborhood, Slice House demonstrates the importance of a design strategy. The architects inherited many restrictions from the outset, ranging from zoning restrictions to the need to develop and test new building techniques. The brief was challenging, but clear: no extravagant materials, just extravagant spaces. The result is a series of living spaces that do not conform to the conventional idea of horizontal and vertical planes. The main design strategy rests on spatial distortions and illusions, in which a series of tilting walls gradually allows the space to fold and unfold, depending on the position of the viewer. The spatial experience allows a dramatic reading of the space, which immediately appears larger and denser than the narrow plot on which it sits.

THE SETTING
Slice House sits on the corner plot at the end of a residential neighborhood. The aerial perspective reveals its linear character and scale in relation to other buildings in the city.

THE LONG SECTION
The relationship between spaces on the lower and upper levels of Slice House are clearly illustrated.

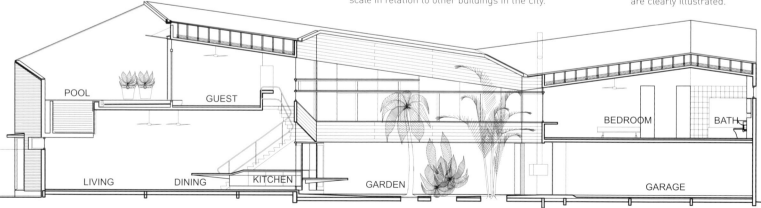

POOL GUEST BEDROOM BATH

LIVING DINING KITCHEN GARDEN GARAGE

SPATIAL COLLISIONS

The linear nature of Slice House allows continuous space to provide a sense of depth, allowing the eye to travel beyond the space it inhabits. The entrance leads us through the living area, then turns into the kitchen, and connects us to the view of the exterior courtyard. Activities are not boxed off or kept separate, so sometimes we may look up to the space above or drop into the pool, to re-emerge below and back into the living space, enjoying the sudden overlap of spaces. These ideas are supported by custom furniture components. The 23-ft. (7-m) kitchen counter is a continuous steel slab, with 6-ft. 6-in. (2-m) cantilevered tables floating off at each end to create a dining table and a courtyard table. The thick steel plate folds up transitionally between the lower dining height and higher work counter. A made-to-fit stainless steel sink has been inserted into the triangle transition underneath.

A continuous table defines the areas of dining, kitchen, and courtyard as its function changes at different points.

GLASS TANK POOL
The swimming pool submerges activity from the upper level down to the lower level in a physical defiance of gravity. Supported by the walls, the glass tank conceals its construction to give the illusion of physical suspension. Visually, the pool is the event generator in the space, giving light, color, and movement.

VISUAL SCALE
Large artworks were commissioned for the space to break up the length of the interior walls and to zone areas without creating physical divisions.

STAIRCASE
A "U" shape stair is ⅜-in. (8-mm) steel plate accordion folded and welded in sections onto the undercarriage beam plates. The thin edge is emphasized in light gray, contrasted with the exposed underside painted in a deep eggplant purple.

Design details are well considered with fixtures and fittings adding to the composition of architectural elements.

OUTDOOR LIVING
The interior courtyard is scaled by exotic palm trees, which provide a visual indication of the undulating height and scale of the building.

FRAMING

There is a playful sense that each area in the house enjoys itself. Framing is used as an architectural tool that captures drama. The swimming pool, located on the upper floor, is the main event generator in the space, and is perceived as a floating block above the living space. It polarizes the attention of viewers in the house when the pool is in use. During the day, it works as a daylight filter, creating different rippled water effects as the quality of light changes. At night, with the pool lights on, it works as a large colored light fixture. Sloping ceilings, corridors that offer different perspectives, folding walls, and floating stairs all become components that add to the rich design vocabulary of this remarkable contemporary dwelling.

MULTIFUNCTIONAL GRILLS
Grills on the windows, courtyard, and onto the terrace have several functions. They provide security and also act as a louver, filtering light into the space. Aesthetically, lighting effects give the interior spaces a transparent quality by making the building flush and continuous as a prism.

BATHROOM

Functional areas are kept simple, efficient, and economical with the plumbing mounted to a single wall to provide maximum space and minimum pipe runs. Practical materials such as ceramic walls and concrete floors and ceilings show a utilitarian approach to functional spaces, without compromising the aesthetic design.

UPPER HALLWAY

On the upper level, a cantilevered hallway creates a linear journey of light and glass, using views onto the interior courtyard, before disappearing into a wrapping ribbon line that flows around the courtyard. The corridor slopes down in height to just over 6 ft. (1.8 m), creating a forced perspective toward the bedroom, making the private area in the house appear further away from the social areas.

DISTRIBUTION OF LIGHT

Sunlight is filtered to the internal spaces through the courtyard and louvers, and through the upper-floor glass-faced swimming pool. Designed as punched holes, the positions of windows are separated to generate pools of light, avoiding bland and even natural lighting. These openings happen at different heights, bringing light and views in unexpected ways into the space.

CIRCULATION

Access to the bedroom, the en-suite, and storage areas is given from both sides of the space to create easy circulation.

5 Professional practice

Professional practice focuses on the integration of key skills into a design portfolio. The portfolio can reflect an individual's attitude, as well as artistic ability and propensity to make good design decisions. This is essential when seeking employment or for using as a reference with clients, and it provides a visual resumé of your work to date that allows you to progress to further study or gain employment.

Key skills in this chapter are personal presentation, design communication, and critical evaluation skills.

Unit 26 | Preparing your portfolio (page 124)

26

Unit 27 | Writing a resumé and cover letter (page 126)

27

Unit 26: Preparing your portfolio

OBJECTIVES
- Produce completed projects to a professional standard
- Learn to prepare, edit, and experiment with different approaches to create the best possible portfolio
- Present individual work to a client or prospective employer

The portfolio is your most important resource—it brings together a coordinated body of your best design work to date. It illustrates the way you think, it draws attention to your ideas, and it shows off your ability to make and communicate design decisions. In this unit you will learn to reflect on the work you have created so far and cast a critical eye over the presentation of your portfolio. Remember that you are using a visual language to communicate and represent your ideas, so clarity is vital.

The portfolio is your professional persona and your passport to the real world. Whether you use it to progress to employment, to further your study, or to show potential clients your range of ideas, it is an important tool to get you moving on.

FORMAT
A portfolio is a book and should have a consistent format. Each page should read the same way, so we view the work in either landscape (horizontal) or portrait (vertical) format. Occasionally there may be some projects that need to be shown in a different way. As most pages will be viewed as a double-page spread, they should be designed as a pair to complement each other.

CONTENT
Most of your work when putting together your portfolio will be editing—an extremely important skill. Your portfolio should not contain every piece of work that you have done to date, only your best projects should be showcased: this is work that is creative, technically excellent, provocative, or engaging.

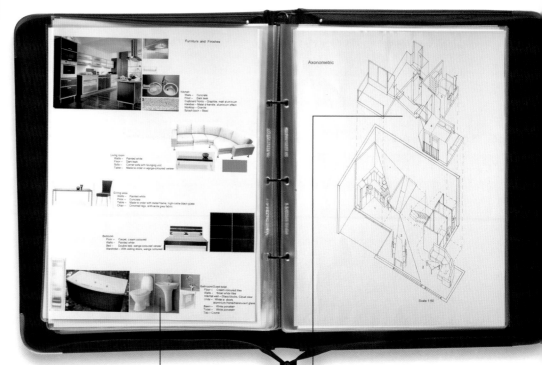

THOROUGH PRESENTATION
Utilizing a 3D drawing, shown together with a sample board, these pages provide good detail regarding layout, use of space, materials, and finishes.

Tearsheets from suppliers' catalogs provide visual contrast to the black and white axonometric drawing on the opposing page.

This presentation layout makes good use of an exploded 3D drawing to show in detail the lower and upper levels of a loft conversion.

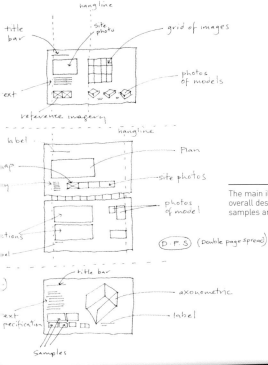

STORYBOARDS
Make sure that you lay out your pages in a storyboard. This shows the sequential order of each page and helps you to decide what goes where, what scale to use, and shows the overall design of key relationships.

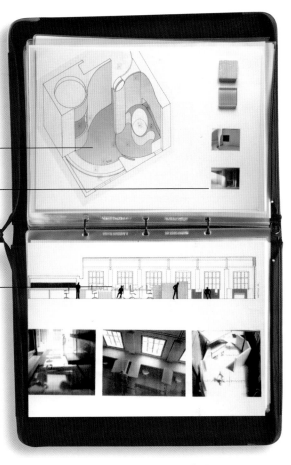

The main illustration gives a good sense of the overall design, and is reinforced by material samples and photographic views of the model.

Thumbnails can also be used to provide a subtext to the main story of the page.

While photographic references are used, the section is expressed as a set of imagined activities.

PRESENTING THE COMPLEX SIMPLY
Although this project looks ambitious at first glance, a well-presented scheme is easily understood.

Sizes of your images can vary according to their importance. The basic rule is scale. Larger images tend to read as key illustrations while smaller images act as references to the main idea.

INFORMATION AND ILLUSTRATION
Consider the relationship between images and words. Text can be used to accompany and support images by providing explanation or information. Alternatively, text can draw attention away from imagery by subverting or contradicting the visual message.

HANG LINES
These are the most basic and fundamental tools for page layout and structure. They help to organize the position of visual imagery and text on the page, but are also vital for creating the language or the narrative of the presentation.

Unit 27: Writing a resumé and cover letter

OBJECTIVES
- Learn to clarify your goals and objectives
- Sell your personal qualities and abilities
- Understand how to design your own personal specification

Your resumé is the first impression a prospective employer will have of your skills, abilities, and previous experiences to date. A well-designed and professionally presented resumé can enhance your chances of success by getting you well on your way, whether you are progressing to employment or to further study. This unit will guide you through the process of writing the best possible resumé—one that will maximize your prospects as well as boosting your self-confidence.

PREPARATION
Before you begin writing your resumé, take some time to clarify your personal goals and objectives. This will help you focus your application by making it relevant and appropriate for your desired outcomes. Consider the career direction in which you wish to move by targeting specific employment opportunities and employers. Phone the organizations you are interested in and find out their recruitment requirements. It is important that your skills and abilities match the job specification you are targeting. Put yourself to the test and consider the reasons why an employer should choose you.

FIRST IMPRESSIONS
Always type your resumé and cover letter and avoid handwriting, which tends to look unprofessional.

CREATING YOUR RESUMÉ
Your objective when writing your resumé is to secure your first steps toward getting an interview. This means highlighting your strengths and playing down your weaknesses. When writing, avoid negative or passive phrases, such as "some experience" or "helped and assisted." Use active words such as "developed," "researched," "supervised," "organized," or "negotiated."

BEING SELECTIVE
Remember to provide the required information, not your life story to date. List your most recent and relevant experience. Being selective and concise results in a more professional and effective resumé. Highlight important information by editing irrelevancies. Tailor your resumé for different applications by adapting the information to suit different job specifications. Don't be afraid to blow your own horn—employers are reassured by confident and strong applicants. Above all, check your resumé for spelling mistakes and grammatical errors.

Consider your resumé as an advertisement that sells your best asset—you. Along with summarizing your personal details, you should strive to present a concise, clear, and attractive document that shows you in a positive light. An effective resumé should therefore be no longer than two sheets of letter paper, the ideal being one sheet, if possible.

FORMAT

There are different types of resumés and therefore different ways of compiling them. The most traditional type is the chronological resumé, which can be adapted to your own style. This format lists personal information, education, qualifications, skills, achievements, and interests. A skills-based resumé is a more effective format for life and work experience. It categorizes and divides important skills into broad areas by identifying the attributes such skills require. Examples include technical skills, managerial skills, teamwork skills, and time management skills. These effectively target the needs and requirements of prospective employers.

PRESENTATION

Your resumé should be of the highest aesthetic standard. Research has shown that resumé communication is 80 percent presentation and 20 percent content. This suggests, correctly, that the market will be competitive, and a prospective employer will have many professional applications to choose from. From the employer's point of view, the initial process is therefore one of elimination. A resumé that is badly designed will be easy to disregard. Creating a visual impact is a must. For text, choose a font that is both legible and attractive. Highlight important phrases to bring attention to critical skills and achievements. Include visuals where possible—even a personal logo or letterhead can make a document look visually stimulating and can be applied to all correspondence to enhance professional credibility. Every detail, right down to the quality of paper you use and your print quality, will be noticed. Remember that a resumé is a snapshot of you, so present yourself well.

COVER LETTER

Every resumé that is sent requires a cover letter. A letter is a personal communication, so avoid using "Dear Sir or Madam." It only takes a phone call to find out the relevant contact name. In the opening paragraph, introduce what you are applying for as well as providing your reasons for wanting to apply. If you are responding to an ad, you should cite the job vacancy and the place you saw it advertised.
If you are writing a speculative letter, you should introduce yourself and identify your current professional position or the relevant stage of your study. Use the rest of the letter to demonstrate background research on the organization and its work. Show that you are eager and interested by providing evidence of specific personal achievements you feel would suit the organization.

STAND OUT

Along with your resumé and cover letter, provide some visual examples of your work. This will help to get you noticed and make you stand out from the rest.

Unit 28: Design roles

OBJECTIVES
- Understand the different design roles
- Understand the anatomy of a design job
- Understand the relevant terminology associated with design roles

A design project requires the professional input of many different people. First there is the client, who will make the project possible; then the design team, which makes the ideas feasible; and finally the myriad subcontractors, who implement and realize the proposal. This unit will explore the anatomy of a design job and consider the different roles required to make a design proposal happen.

MEETINGS
Meetings are the lifeblood of decision making, particularly within a large team. Good communication enables information to flow down the design hierarchy.

Tackling a project can be both exciting and deeply rewarding. Designing is a social activity, and as a designer you will learn to work with many different professionals. Any project that you work on will always be a team effort, so it is important to pull the right team together to get the best possible result.

THE CLIENT
A client can be an individual or a company, a government office, or some other organization. Your client is the most important person in the anatomy of the job, and therefore sits at the top of the hierarchy. The client makes the job possible, and will have ultimate say over the process. All decisions concerning the design will have to be relayed to the client and agreed upon before they can be passed down the chain to be implemented.

THE DESIGNER/DESIGN TEAM
As designer, you may undertake many different roles and responsibilities within the design process. You may be seen as a facilitator, translator, diplomat, and director, translating the client's wishes into a coherent and effective design solution. Once appointed, a designer/design team is expected to conform to the professional code of conduct that governs the standards related to the practice of design. Once the designer/team comes up with the initial sketch design, they will then require the services of the quantity surveyor.

MATERIALS MANAGER

The materials or purchasing manager (left) is responsible for advising the design team and realizing the design proposal.

MATERIALS MANAGER

The materials or purchasing manager (also called a "quantity surveyor" in the UK and Australia) studies architectural and engineering drawings and specifications to prepare a bill of materials, which lists the individual components required to realize the design proposal in the most effective way. This person checks on design changes to access their effects on costs, and may prepare monthly cash-flow projections and tax depreciation schedules for clients. A materials manager is a must for large-scale design projects, but can be effectively employed on an hourly rate for smaller projects.

MAIN CONTRACTOR

The main contractor is directly responsible to the client and the design team, and will also work alongside the quantity surveyor. The job consists of directing the work onsite to schedule and within budget. The contractor may also be in charge of subcontracting out the work to a team of specialist subcontractors. These may be chosen either by the contractor alone or jointly by all three parties.

SPECIALIST CONSULTANTS

Specialist consultants are appointed to advise the designers in areas of technical knowledge, including mechanical and electrical heating, ventilation, electrical fittings or lighting, and information technology (products and services). Structural engineers may be required to advise on structural changes and major alterations.

1. STANDARD MINOR WORKS

```
        CLIENT

Designer ←————→ Contractor
```

2. MANAGEMENT CONTRACTOR

```
         CLIENT

Designer ←————→ Contractor

                 Subcontractors
```

3. CONSTRUCTION MANAGEMENT

```
         CLIENT

Designer ←——→ Contractor

              Subcontractor
```

WAYS OF WORKING
1 The simplest project entails designer and contractor reporting to the client.

2 Larger-scale works ideally entail the contractor briefing the sub-contractors.

3 From a client point-of-view, the least-preferred option in which they brief all parties.

Unit 29: The design industry

OBJECTIVES
- Understand the industry
- Research the marketplace
- Learn to promote yourself

Working in the design industry may be your end goal but before you reach this stage you will need to research the field, meet professionals, seek advice, and build a network of industry contacts. Being prepared takes time, energy, and effort, but once you establish a foothold within the industry, the possibilities are endless. This unit sets out important guidelines to help you start out in the field of interior design. Prospective employers, possible routes to employment, and methods of marketing are all covered to get you started.

WHERE TO START?

Starting out can be both exciting and daunting, but the process of finding a job can be a real eye opener. Gauging the nature of the industry and the attitude of employers, and becoming accustomed to the competitive climate, is a tough learning curve, but remember that starting out is always the most difficult part of the process. Be prepared to take the challenges in your stride, and the results can be rewarding.

WHAT DO INTERIOR DESIGNERS DO?

As simple as the question may sound, there is often a lot of confusion surrounding the actual role of an interior designer. Interior design is a homeless discipline and sits somewhere between product design and architecture. This is actually an advantage, however, and enables designers to progress into a series of related jobs, including decorating and styling, theater or set design, retail and commercial design, exhibition design, residential design and property development, furniture design and refurbishment, landscape design, and architecture.

RETAIL DESIGN

Retail projects have a short shelf-life, a high turnover, and are often closely aligned to fashion.

WHAT SKILLS DO INTERIOR DESIGNERS REQUIRE?

The role of the designer is a complex one, which requires many interpersonal skills. Designers on the whole are facilitators. They make projects happen by communicating clearly and by building good working relationships. In the current design climate, most designers are accustomed to working in a multidisciplinary way. Working collaboratively with other creative people, such as graphic or product designers, architects, or artists, can generate real opportunities to move beyond your own skill set. These can be extremely profitable relationships, as clients often require many different people in a project.

HOW DO INTERIOR DESIGNERS GET WORK?

Most methods of finding employment are through networking. Interior design positions are rarely advertised, so seeking out work is a must. In the first instance it is a good idea to contact large companies who have a high turnover of staff, as they will be most likely to have vacancies.

FREELANCE OR PRACTICE?

Working freelance and setting up a practice are very similar in many ways: establishing a practice can be seen as taking freelance status one step further, and therefore constituting a bigger commitment. It is best to work first as a freelancer and set up a practice once you have completed a few projects.

Going freelance

ADVANTAGES
- Low overhead costs; can work from home
- You can deduct a lot of costs for taxes: for example, your work phone bill
- You can use your own bank account and avoid business banking charges
- You can take on as much work as you wish

DISADVANTAGES
- Home- and work-life may clash in terms of time and space
- Less regular working hours—sometimes work may be scarce, at others you may be very busy
- Work, samples, and brochures will take up space at home, and can cause a mess
- You may struggle to appear as professional as contemporaries who are employed or running their own practice

Setting up a practice

ADVANTAGES
- You will immediately appear more professional
- Your clients can visit you in your office
- You could be able to charge more for your work
- It is easier to get trade accounts with suppliers
- You can open a business bank account with overdraft facilities
- You can more easily keep to regular office hours, and leave work behind you at the end of the day
- You can work with a business partner (preferably with complementary skills) to share decision-making and stress

DISADVANTAGES
- Accounts are more complicated than being a freelancer, and accountants will charge you more
- Greater overhead costs involved in running an office

DIVERSITY
The commercial design industry opens up the designer to diverse environments and requirements.

Alternatively, finding work in a small practice gives the designer a more responsible and close-knit relationship within the company. Whatever you choose, it is advisable to spend at least a year at a company in order to gain crucial skills, understand how design jobs are run, and build your confidence before going freelance or setting up your own business. Remember that there is a lot to learn. Gain as much experience as you can, whether it's paid or unpaid work. Make your mistakes at someone else's expense before you set up on your own!

HOW DO INTERIOR DESIGNERS MAKE CONTACTS IN THE INDUSTRY?

The design world is small. Once you begin working in the industry you will quickly meet other designers and get to know most of the design companies and practices. It is in your interest to market yourself as widely as possible. Opportunities can come when you least expect them. In the beginning, it may be a good idea to enter competitions as a way of promoting your work, as well as building up your portfolio. When visiting a prospective employer, create a marketing pack with examples of your best work and a resumé (see Unit 27: Writing a resumé and cover letter). Talking is the best way of networking, exchanging ideas, and making contacts. Visit trade fairs and take advantage of membership organizations as a way of meeting people informally. While you are looking, keep up-to-date by visiting museums and galleries, reading design magazines and trade journals, and keep on producing work. Enthusiasm, determination, and confidence will pay off. It may be a slow process—but don't give up!

VARIETY
Projects can range from complete environments to the design of bespoke furniture pieces.

PROFESSIONAL TRAINING, ACCREDITATION, AND REGISTRATION

The standard for interior design education is a bachelor's degree from a Foundation for Interior Design Education Research (FIDER) accredited university. To become certified or licensed, designers must pass the National Council for Interior Design Qualifying (NCIDQ) exam. The two primary professional organizations in the U.S. for interior designers are the American Society of Interior Designers (ASID) and the International Interior Design Association (IIDA).

Unit 30 : Setting up on your own

OBJECTIVES
- Develop a business strategy
- Weigh up the pros and cons
- Create a good foundation of skills

If you become a freelance designer you will have the flexibility to work for both individuals and practices, while setting up your own practice. Becoming the boss means that the onus is on you—you must be organized, efficient, and prepared to take responsibility for the financial highs as well as the lows. This unit gives you advice about the pros and cons of setting up on your own, and considers the practical skills you will need in order to do well.

COMMUNICATION
Keep a good line of communication open with everyone from the bank manager to the client.

PROFESSIONAL EXPERIENCE
By the time you set up your own practice you need to be confident, not just in your skills as a designer, but that you can make a success of the business. Experience working for an established design company prior to setting up your own practice is invaluable, and working for a range of companies, from the small design firm to the corporate giant, will give you a broad understanding of how you want to run your own business. Even if you get offered private work early on, working for a company will allow you to see how the business is run.

FINDING CLIENTS
A good portfolio will inspire a client, but first you have to find one. Inform everyone you know that you are now an interior designer, as clients arrive via the strangest recommendations, and word of mouth can be a valuable asset.

Use suppliers and showrooms to advertise your services. Leave cards and flyers in relevant shops, register your practice in the phonebook, advertise your services in design trade magazines, and introduce yourself to as many people in the industry as possible. Recruitment agencies and design organizations can be a good way of generating work quickly and establishing yourself within the marketplace.

ESTABLISHING AN IDENTITY
A good design firm should have a clear identity, and clients should choose it because they sympathize with its design language. If you naturally have a particularly strong approach, then run with it. This way you are more likely to become renowned in the industry. It is likely that

prospective clients will also recognize this as a strength in your work and will be more confident when employing you. If you enjoy undertaking a range of diverse projects, then use this to your advantage when attracting new clients. It's important to enjoy the challenges of your design projects, since each offers its own design opportunities, but it's also good to have a strategy. In the short term, taking on any project that comes along can usefully widen a designer's experience, but as you gain experience you will soon learn that some jobs just don't inspire you. In the long term move away from inappropriate design jobs and avoid similar recommendations that lead you to being stuck in a field that doesn't suit your practice or your aspirations.

SKILLS REQUIRED

A freelance designer needs to be able to interpret a client's requirements and bring them together. Every project is different and, more importantly, no two clients are the same. You will soon discover that much of the success of a finished job depends on your rapport with the client and vice versa. So, to begin with, you need to be able to listen to what the client wants, and communicate how you plan to make that happen.

The design and construction industry is built of many parts. Being good in all areas is ideal if you want to run your own practice; however, understanding your strengths and your role within a team are also great qualities. While you don't need the specialist knowledge that a construction contractor has, understanding the limitations and opportunities of techniques and being able to communicate them is an advantage

Your knowledge will increase with each job, but in the meantime you should not be afraid to ask the professionals. A good contractor will be happy to advise you, and if your client asks an awkward question, simply tell them that you will look into it and get back to them.

MAKING IT WORK

Setting up on your own sounds exciting and liberating, but it is not all glamor and glory. There are a few more mundane aspects of the job and qualities you need to embrace to make it work. To begin with, don't be afraid to compromise or look for a middle way, and do be prepared to do the "boring stuff."

Being a good all-rounder is a distinct advantage in the business, but everyone has their strengths and weaknesses. Make sure that you know yours, and make use of good teamwork by realizing what you can't do yourself and finding the right person to do it.

Glossary

Axonometric
A three-dimensional drawing depicting a model view of an interior space by projecting up the heights of a true plan

Bubble diagram
A spatial diagram showing the relationship between spaces and their intended activities

Building regulations
A set of codes and standards that are based on health and safety requirements to ensure good design practice

CAD
Computer-aided design programs used for drafting, modeling, and simulating spatial ideas in the design process

Cavities
The inbetween spaces and voids that help to expose the edges or profile of solids

Cut-through points
The points at which the cut-line or a section is taken, determining the view of the interior, either as a plan or section view

Concept board
A two-dimensional visual presentation of an idea or set of ideas created in the initial stages of the project for the client

Cone of vision
Represents the view that can be seen in a perspective drawing before it becomes distorted

Contractor
A specialist who works for the design team and the client to realize, construct, and manage the final design on site

Dead loads
The weight of materials and structures that do not move

Design brief
A set of aims given by the client to define the parameters of the design task

Design criteria
A set of important objectives that the designer wishes to achieve

Design language
An approach adopted to inform the design and describe an aesthetic narrative with material relationships

Design process
A set of design stages that the designer will undergo to carry out and complete the project

Design proposal
A written document that outlines how the designer will carry out and achieve the design scheme

Design scheme
A final design that reconfigures a given space to achieve a client brief

Design strategy
A set of criteria driven by a central idea or concept

Design team
A group of skilled professionals that can include structural engineers, quantity surveyors, electrical and mechanical engineers, interior designers, and architects

Dimension lines
A set of lines that indicates the position of dimensions on technical or freehand survey drawings

Drawing conventions
A visual language that is employed by designers to depict and communicate spatial ideas in both two- and three-dimensional drawing

Ecological design
Sustainable design that uses recycled materials, low technology, and conserves energy by using solar or wind power

Elevation
A two-dimensional drawing depicting the exterior facade of an object or a building

Ergonomics
The relationship between a person and their practical environment where dimensions are crucial to individual use and health

Facade
The face or front of a building

Freehand
Drawn by hand without the aid of technical equipment

HVAC system
Heating, ventilation, and air conditioning

Interior decoration
The refurbishment and styling of interior spaces

Interior decorator
A skilled professional responsible for revitalizing interior spaces according to intended activities usually including the specification and sourcing of furniture, upholstery, window dressings, color schemes, lighting, and furniture layouts

Interior design
The spatial and structural design of interior environments

Interior designer
A skilled professional who is responsible for designing interior environments that accommodate the user, either by modifying what already exists or by providing an entirely new program for the space. Interior designers usually work alongside a design team to realize a project

Jig
An object to hold pieces accurately in place when glueing

Lighting plan
A plan drawing that shows the position and types of lighting used in an interior scheme

Line weights
A drawing convention used in the depiction of two-dimensional drawings to convey depth and material properties

Live loads
The weight of people and furniture; elements that can be added or taken away from the completed design and therefore must be taken into account in the building's construction

Load bearing
Architectural components that carry, support, or channel loads to the ground

Micro building
A small-scale building or form

Minimalist design
A multifunctional approach to design making it both flexible and practical

Orthographic
Two-dimensional views in the form of plans, sections, and elevations that keep the scale and proportion of dimensions consistent

Pair of strings
A step support used to construct a staircase in model making

Partition
A structure that divides a space into parts

Perspective
A three-dimensional view of an object, interior, or building that is constructed according to eye-level

Plan
A two-dimensional drawing showing the view above an interior space once it has been cut at waist height

Planning
A process of working out, coordinating, and organizing a given space

Portfolio
A comprehensive body of work that showcases projects, personal ability, and professional design skills

Presentation model
A model that employs realistic materials and finishes in order to convey the atmosphere of a completed design scheme

Proportional system
A system that achieves harmony by establishing the ratio of one measurement or proportion to another

Rabbet
A step-shaped channel cut along the edge or face of a material to receive the edge or tongue of another material

Recycling
A process of revitalizing existing materials in order to reduce energy and wastage

Sample board
A visual presentation of materials used within the design scheme depicting furniture, fixtures, fittings and finishes

Scale
The given size of something, whether enlarged, reduced or kept true

Section
A two-dimensional view of an interior once it has been vertically cut either through the length or the width of the building

Sketch model
A loose physical model of a spatial idea using economic materials and quick processes

Solids
Architectural composition wherein materials in building are used to depict mass as a whole

Spatial
The architectural experience of space

Spider diagram
A diagram used for brainstorming different ideas and alternatives

Strength/weight ratio
The relationship of the weight of a material to its strength

Sustainability
Achieved by the use of materials that are from a renewable source, do not harm the environment, or endanger ecological balance

Survey
The process of measuring a space in order to gather data for the construction of technical drawings

Technical drawing
A method of drawing using technical equipment together with drawing conventions to produce accurate scale drawings

Vanishing point
The point at which all lines vanish or diminish in a perspective drawing

Resources

INTERIOR DESIGN ORGANIZATIONS

American Society of Interior Designers (ASID)

ASID is one of two primary US professional organizations, the other being the International Interior Design Association (see below). ASID has 38,000 members who strive to advance interior design through education, advocacy, community building, and outreach.
608 Massachusetts Ave NE, Washington, DC, 20002, USA
www.asid.org

British Interior Design Association (BIDA)

Originally formed in 2002 through the Interior Decorators and Designers Association (IDDA) and the International Interior Design Association (IIDA, UK chapter), this professional body for interior designers continues to promote high professional standards. It provides course information, member's links, and student membership.
1 / 4 Chelsea Harbour Design Centre, Chelsea Harbour, London SW 10 OXE, UK
www.bida.org

British Interior Textiles Association (BITA)

This association represents and promotes the UK contract and domestic furnishings and interior textile trade. The online product and supplier guide is useful and is also accompanied by a trend guide.
5 Portland Place, London, W1B 1PW, UK
www.interiortextiles.co.uk

The Chartered Society of Designers (CSD)

CSD is the world's largest chartered body of professional designers and is unique in representing designers of all disciplines. CSD is governed by royal charter and as such its members are obliged to practice to the highest professional standards. In so doing, it seeks to secure and promote a professional body of designers and regulate and control their practice for the benefit of industry and the public.
5 Bermondsey Exchange, 179-181 Bermondsey St., London SE1 3UW, UK
www.csd.org.uk

Design4Design

This comprehensive and valuable directory of design related disciplines gives events, provides a searchable database, and lists jobs in design for interior, furniture, and product designers.
ETP Ltd, 6 - 14 Underwood Street, London, N1 7JQ UK
www.design4design.com

The International Interior Design Association (IIDA)

A professional networking and educational association with over 10,000 members throughout nine regions and with 30 chapters around the world, IIDA is committed to enhancing the quality of life through excellence in design and the advancement of design through knowledge.
13-122 Merchandise Mart, Chicago, IL, 60654-1104, USA
www.iida.org

National Council for Interior Design Qualification, Inc. (NCIDQ)

The NCIDQ certifies interior designers in North America by way of the NCIDQ examination. Passing the examination is a requirement for interior designers wishing to register in many states or provinces, and for every designer applying for professional membership.
1200 18th Street NW, Suite 1001, Washington, DC 20036-2506
http://www.ncidq.org

INTERIOR DESIGN COLLEGES

The following North American universities are accredited by the Foundation of Interior Design Education Research (www.fider.org).

USA

Arizona State University, Tempe
Interior Design Program
College of Design
Tempe, Arizona 85287-2105
480-965-4135
http://www.asu.edu/caed/SOD/index.htm

University of Cincinnati
School of Architecture and Interior Design
P.O. Box 210016
Cincinnati OH 45221-0016
513-556-6426
www.said.uc.edu

Cornell University, Ithaca
Interior Design Program
Department of Design and Environmental Analysis
College of Human Ecology
145 Martha Van Rensselaer Hall
Ithaca, NY 14853
607-255-2168
dea.human.cornell.edu

Kansas State University
Interior Design Program
Department of Apparel, Textiles and Interior Design
College of Human Ecology
225 Justin Hall
Manhattan, KS 66506
785-532-1317
www.k-state.edu

University of Oregon
School of Architecture and Allied Arts
105 Lawrence Hall
541-346-3631
Eugene, OR 97403-1206
aaa.uoregon.edu

Bibliography

Pratt Institute
Interior Design Department
School of Art and Design
Pratt Studios 21
200 Willoughby Ave.
Brooklyn, NY 11205
718-636-3630
www.pratt.edu

Syracuse University
Interior Design Program
School of Art and Design
College of Visual & Performing
Arts
Syracuse, NY 13244
315.443.2455
vpa.syr.edu/index.html

CANADA
University of Manitoba,
Winnipeg, MB
Department of Interior Design
204.474.9458
E-mail:
miyahar@cc.umanitoba.ca
Web:
http://www.umanitoba.ca/archite
cture/id

Ryerson University
The School of Interior Design
350 Victoria Street
Toronto Ontario M5B 2K3
Canada
416-979-5188
http://www.ryerson.ca

Adler, David
**Metric Handbook,
Planning and Design Data**
(2nd Edition) Architectural Press,
(1999)

Adler, David, and Tutt,
Patricia, eds.
**New Metric Handbook:
Planning and Design Data**
Architectural Press, (1992)

Ashcroft, Roland
**Construction for Interior
Designers**
Longman, Art and Design, (1992)

Baden-Powell, Charlotte
Architect's Pocket Book
Architectural Press, (2001)

Ching, Francis
Architectural Graphics
Van Nostrand Reinhold

Ching, Francis
Design Drawing
Van Nostrand Reinhold (1998)

Ching, Francis
Interior Design Illustrated
Van Nostrand Reinhold (2000)

Gaventa, Sarah
Concrete Design
Mitchell Beazley, (2001)

Georman, Jean
**Detailing Light: Integrated
Lighting Solutions for
Residential and Contract Design**
Whitney Library of Design, (1995)

Hohauser, Sanford
**Architectural and Interior
Models**
(2nd Edition), Van Nostrand
Reinhold, (1982)

Itten, Johannes
**The Art of Color: The Subjective
Experience and Objective
Rationale of Color**
Van Norstrand Reinhold, (1961)

Jiricna, Eva, Staircases
Laurence King Publishing,
(2001)

Kilmer and Kilmer
Designing Interiors,
Wadsworth Publishing, (1994)

Martin, Cat
The Surface Texture Book
Gardners Books, (2005)

McGowan, Maryrose, and Kruse,
Kelsey
Interior Graphic Standards
John Wiley, (2004)

Neufert, Ernst, and
Neufert, Peter
Architect's Data (3rd Edition)
Blackwell Science, (2000)

Nijsse, Rob,
**Glass in Structures: Elements,
Concepts, Designs**
Birkhauser, (2003)

Reekie, Fraser, revised by
Tony McCarthy
Reekie's Architectural Drawing
Architectural Press, 1995

Szalapaj, Peter
**CAD Principles for Architectural
Design: Analytic Approaches to
Computational Representation
of Architectural Form**
Architectural Press, (2001)

Trudeau, N
**Professional Modelmaking: A
Handbook of Techniques and
Materials for Architects and
Designers**
Whitney Library of Design, (1995)

van Onna, Edwin
**Material World: Innovative
Structures and Finishes for
Interiors**
Birkhauser, (2003)

Yee, R
**Architectural Drawing: A Visual
Compendium of Types and
Methods**
Wiley, (2004)

Hoehauser, Sanford
**Architectural and Interior
Models: Design and
Construction**
Van Nostrand Reinhold, (1984)

Index

DEDICATION
For Bilge, with all my love

Credits

The author and Quarto would like to thank the following students from Chelsea College of Art and Design for their contribution:

Leo Bartlett, Oliver Brown, Nikki Bruun-meyer, Toby Burgess, Annabelle Campbell, Ruth Canning, Lisa Cooper, Charlotte Dewar, Mikaela Dyhlen, Niti Gourisaria, Ussmaa Gulsar, Chisato Haruyama, Caroline Howard, Tamsin Hurst, Go Immamura, Jacinda Jones, Nicola Lichfield, Loucas Louca, Karen Malacarne, Laura Matthews, Glenn Mccance, Lisa Moss, Annika Nordblom, Mayumi Saigan, Abigail Szeto, Hiroko Tanaka

CASE STUDY ILLUSTRATIONS
Leith Adjina, Nem Adjina, John Fieldhouse, Brooke Fieldhouse Associates and Duncan McNeill Imaging, Rachel and Jonathan Forster, Forster Inc., Chris Procter and Fernando Rihl, Procter-Rihl

MODEL MAKING
George Rome Innes

PERSPECTIVES
Janey Sharratt

LIGHTING
Jayne Fisher

CAD
Anthony Parsons, Chris Procter and Fernando Rihl, Robert Bell, Sally Wilson

PROFESSIONAL PRACTICE
Rachel and Jonathan Forster, Lyndall Fernie and Stuart Knock, Chris Procter, and Fernando Rihl

Quarto would also like to thank and acknowledge the following for supplying photographs reproduced in this book:

Key: t = top, b = bottom, l = left, r = right

32-33t Michel Tcherevkoff; The Image Bank/Getty, 68-69t The Special Photographers Company/Getty, 82-83t Pete Turner; The Image Bank/Getty, 93 Chinch Gryniewicz, Ecoscene/Corbis, 96 PhotoDisc, Inc., 97l Gl-o Interiors LLP www.gl-o.com, 97r, 98, 99 VOS SOLUTIONS LTD www.vossolutions.com, 101 Jan Baldwin/Narratives, 122-123t Marc Trigalou, Photographer's Choice/Getty.

All other photographs and illustrations are the copyright of Quarto Publishing plc. While every effort has been made to credit contributors, Quarto would like to apologize should there have been any omissions or errors - and would be pleased to make the appropriate correction for future editions of the book.